Ancoats

Cradle of industrialisation

Ancoats

Cradle of industrialisation

Michael E Rose with Keith Falconer and Julian Holder

Published by English Heritage, The Engine House, Fire Fly Avenue, Swindon SN2 2EH
www.english-heritage.org.uk
English Heritage is the Government's statutory adviser on all aspects of the historic environment.

© English Heritage 2011

First published 2011

ISBN 978 1 84802 027 6
Product code 51453

British Library Cataloguing in Publication data
A CIP catalogue record for this book is available from the British Library.

For more information about English Heritage images, contact Archives Research Services, The Engine House, Fire Fly Avenue, Swindon SN2 2EH; telephone (01793) 414600.

Brought to publication by Joan Hodsdon, Publishing, English Heritage.

Typeset in ITC Charter 9.25 on 13pt

Photographs by James O Davies and Peter Williams
Aerial photographs by Dave MacLeod
Graphics by Allan Adams, Nigel Fradgley and Kate Parsons
Edited by Merle Read
Page layout by Pauline Hull

Printed in the UK by Colourhouse

Front cover
Mills on Rochdale Canal.
[DP058591]

Inside front cover
The glazed atrium at McConnel's mills.
[DP058608]

Frontispiece
The communal 'Heart of Ancoats', St Peter's Church. A new public space, Cutting Room Square to the west of the church, provides a centrepoint for the local community and visitors. Five art installations by Dan Dubowitz surround the square.
[DP136561]

This book is dedicated to Robina McNeil (1950–2007)

A tireless champion of Manchester's industrial heritage

Contents

Acknowledgements

The production of this book was very much a partnership between Heritage Works Buildings Preservation Trust (formerly Ancoats Buildings Preservation Trust) and English Heritage. Part-funded through the ABPT's Murrays' Mills permanent repair project, the book contributes to the Trust's work in helping to interpret our heritage to a broad audience and involving local people in the regeneration of their neighbourhood. Heritage Works are very grateful to the Heritage Lottery Fund and the Northwest Regional Development Agency for their contribution to the funding of the production of the initial text. Kate Dickson, Michael Hebbert, Lorna Tittle and Terry Wyke of Heritage Works ably assisted the main author, Michael Rose, in the preparation of much of the initial text, while Julian Holder and Keith Falconer of English Heritage contributed the remainder.

All three authors wish to thank the staff of Manchester Archives and Local Studies section; Chetham's Library; Ian Miller of Oxford Archaeology North, for information and images of the main mills in Ancoats; and Lee Gregory of the University of Manchester Archaeology Unit, for sharing his research on housing in Ancoats.

Julian Holder would like to thank Paul Butler of Paul Butler Associates, Lyn Fenton and Stefan Brzozowski, formerly of New East Manchester Ltd, Clare Hartwell of the Architectural History Practice, Warren Marshall formerly of Manchester City Council, and Ken Moth formerly of the Building Design Partnership.

The authors are also grateful for the assistance and support provided by their English Heritage colleagues in the Swindon, York and Manchester offices. Thanks are due to Joan Hodsdon for providing sound advice throughout the production process. The terrestrial photographs were taken by James O Davies and Peter Williams and the air photographs by Dave McCleod, while Ursula Dugard-Craig assisted with the research and marshalled the photographic input. Thanks are also due to Allan Adams for the introductory location map and for later updates to the maps, to Nigel Fradgley for the Loom Street plan, to Kate Parsons for the end map, to John Cattell and Mike Williams for their comments on the text, to the NMR photographic section for digital images of historical material, and finally to Henry Owen-John and Andrew Davison of the North West region for their continued support.

Foreword

Ancoats holds a very special place in industrial heritage, not just in England but in all industrialised countries. In a period of little over 50 years from the late 18th century, a rural landscape on the eastern outskirts of Manchester was transformed into one of the most densely developed industrial landscapes in the world – the pioneer industrial suburb of the Industrial Revolution. This book tells the story of that transformation and its aftermath, and shows why due regard for the surviving manifestations of these momentous events is so important.

By the second half of the 20th century the district had become a ghost of its former self, its mills and factories closed, its canals derelict, its religious and institutional buildings in ruins, and its communities dispersed. The loss of such a significant proportion of Ancoats' industrial heritage – mills, factories, institutional buildings and industrial housing – through disuse, neglect and demolition, frequently without any form of permanent record, was of national concern.

By the early 1990s that loss, and the threat of even more losses, brought about a campaign to safeguard and revitalise the heritage that had survived in the heartland district to the north of the Rochdale Canal. Working with Manchester City Council, a loose coalition of local and national conservation and regeneration bodies – Ancoats Buildings Preservation Trust (now Heritage Works Buildings Preservation Trust), English Heritage, English Partnerships, the Ancoats Urban Village Company, Eastside Regeneration (now part of New East Manchester) and, latterly, the Northwest Regional Development Agency and the Heritage Lottery Fund – has striven to protect and fund the restoration of key buildings in this area. All the partners in this undertaking are committed to the enhancement of the Ancoats historic environment, and this book is a building block in that process.

Baroness Andrews
Chair of English Heritage

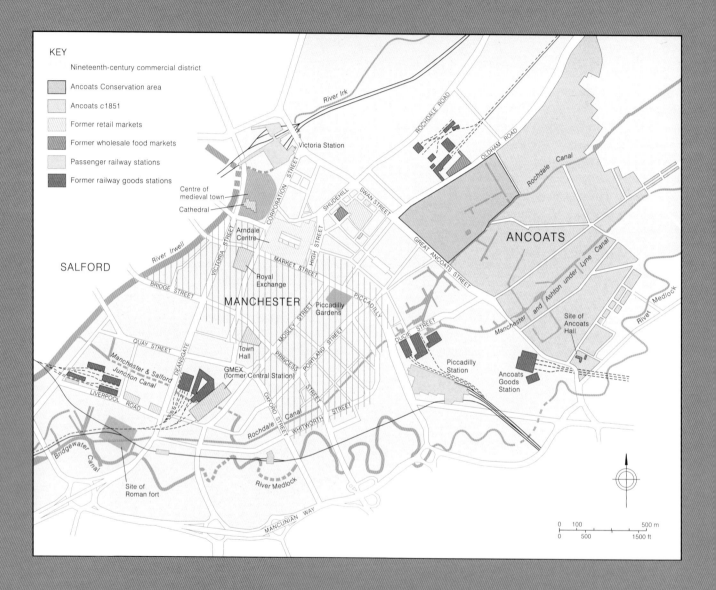

KEY

Nineteenth-century commercial district

Ancoats Conservation area

Ancoats c1851

Former retail markets

Former wholesale food markets

Passenger railway stations

Former railway goods stations

River Irk

Victoria Station

Centre of
medieval town

Cathedral

Arndale
Centre

Royal
Exchange

River Irwell

BRIDGE STREET

SALFORD

MANCHESTER

VICTORIA STREET

CORPORATION STREET

SHUDEHILL

SWAN STREET

HIGH STREET

MARKET STREET

ROCHDALE ROAD

OLDHAM ROAD

Rochdale Canal

ANCOATS

GREAT ANCOATS STREET

Manchester and Ashton under Lyne Canal

River Medlock

Piccadilly
Gardens

PICCADILLY

Site of
Ancoats Hall

MOSLEY STREET

PRINCESS STREET

PORTLAND STREET

DUCIE STREET

Town
Hall

GMEX
(former Central Station)

QUAY STREET

DEANSGATE

Manchester & Salford
Junction Canal

LIVERPOOL ROAD

OXFORD STREET

STREET

WHITWORTH STREET

Rochdale Canal

Piccadilly
Station

Ancoats
Goods
Station

Bridgewater Canal

Site of
Roman fort

River Medlock

MANCUNIAN WAY

0   100   500 m
0   500   1500 ft

1

Introduction

The story of Ancoats is much more than the story of canals and mills combining to create the first industrial landscape based on steam power – it encompasses the rise (and eventual decline) of a complete industrial suburb which has a unique place in the history of both global industrialisation and urbanisation. Its multi-storied steam-driven cotton mills, which had been hailed as a marvel of the late Georgian era and featured on the itineraries of European and American visitors to England, had become a magnet for immigrant workers whose housing and living conditions were to be condemned by social commentators a generation later. Ancoats' population and its industrial influence had peaked by the middle of the 19th century, and although its mills continued to expand into the early 20th century, this was against a background of recognised social deprivation, depopulation and slum clearance.

Understanding how Ancoats assumed its present form is crucial to the success of managing change. The account of the development of the pioneer steam-driven mills, of supply of sub-standard housing speculatively built to house the influx of workers, of the working conditions of those communities, and of the provision of buildings of religious and social concern is the stuff of the earlier chapters of the book. These cover the greater Ancoats district, embracing both the Rochdale and Ashton canals, and most of the historical commentaries and population statistics refer to this wider area (Fig 1). They outline the changing ethnic and employment composition of the communities and, through its buildings, illustrate the evolution of the district's distinctive landscape brought about by these changes.

The later chapters deal with the decline of Ancoats as an industrial powerhouse and with its ongoing rescue as a precious part of the nation's industrial heritage. To inform this rescue many of the surviving mill buildings have been recently studied in great detail, and, through archaeological investigation, many of the cleared sites have yielded up evidence both of early mill development and of the changes in housing types over a period of two centuries. This work was mainly undertaken through the provisions of the Planning Acts by Oxford Archaeology North and the University of Manchester

The location of Ancoats, showing its 1851 area on the periphery of Manchester.

ADSHEAD'S TWENTY FOUR Illustrated Maps OF THE TOWNSHIP OF MANCHESTER DIVIDED INTO MUNICIPAL WARDS CORRECTED TO THE 1ST MAY. 1851

Published by Joseph Adshead, No. 45 George Street Manchester

Scale of Yards

TOWNSHIP OF MANCHESTER No 24

Figure 1 (opposite)
Adshead's index map, identifying Ancoats as New Cross
Ward. Bounded by the broad Oldham Road, Great
Ancoats Street and the River Medlock, it comprises much
of the eastern quadrant of the 'Township of Manchester'.
Its symbiotic relationship to the Rochdale and Ashton
canals and their numerous branches is graphically evident.
[Detail from Adshead 1851 No. 24. Courtesy of Digital
Archives Association]

Figure 2 (below)
Ancoats Conservation Area, designated
in 1989 to counter the impending loss of character
caused by widespread demolition of early buildings.
It represents only a quarter of the historic Ancoats area.
[NMR 20787/27]

Archaeology Unit, and its subsequent synthesis has amply demonstrated the potential of such survey. For some sections of the text the authors have leaned heavily on this work, and they would wish to acknowledge the information and assistance so freely given.

While the historical background covers the wider Ancoats district, the book's main focus, particularly in the final chapter, is on the current developments in the Ancoats Conservation Area: given the losses elsewhere, this is perforce the subject of most of the modern illustrations (Fig 2). In the mid-19th century a *Morning Chronicle* supplement entitled *The Cotton Metropolis: Manchester in 1849* (quoted above) observed that the changes to the Ancoats landscape were dramatic even by Manchester's own standards – the same could be said about the present changes a century and a half later.

2

Pre-industrial Ancoats

The origins of Ancoats are obscure. An area of land stretching north and east from the edge of the town of Manchester, it was one of the 8 medieval 'hamlets' of the town and later one of its 31 townships, with a constable responsible to the Court Leet. Land grants from the 13th century onwards mention 'Annecotes' or 'Antecotes', a name which may refer to an area of opened enclosures (cotes), or to cottages (cotes) close to water (am), or, in another explanation, to the cottage (cote) of a Saxon named Anna. It was a piece of open land with scattered farms and cottages, with the only building of note, at the extreme east of the district, being the half-timbered Ancoats Hall (Fig 3), and was, as Bruton noted, 'beautifully situated above the Medlock with lovely views over green wooded country'. In 1596 the Hall was purchased from the Byrom family by Oswald Mosley, and for the next two centuries it became the seat of the Mosleys, lords of the manor of Manchester. It was later purchased by the mill owner George Murray, and substantially altered into a brick-built Victorian mansion.

By the 1780s – when the Mosley family left their Ancoats seat for one at Rolleston in Staffordshire – Manchester, as the historian Axon commented a century later, 'was throwing out its long arms and the pleasant gardens and fine old Hall were now almost in its grimy clasp'. Rapid trade and population growth in Manchester made the cheaper vacant land in its adjoining districts attractive to industrialists and to house-builders. Late 18th-century maps of

(Opposite)
New Cross and the Crown & Kettle public house c 1800.
[Detail from Manchester Archives and Local Studies m03621]

Figure 3 (right)
Ancoats Old Hall.
[P Rothwell 1794. Manchester Archives and Local Studies m80383]

Figure 4 (opposite)
Pre-canal Ancoats with an emerging speculative street pattern. Properties line Newton Lane (Oldham Road) and Ancoats Lane, but the rest of the area is still quite rural, with Shooter's Brook to the south-east.
[Detail from Laurent 1793. Courtesy of Digital Archives Association]

Figure 5 (below)
Ancoats street names, now peeling but extant. Some personal, some industrial and some rural, they are evocative of the character of Ancoats.
[DP058573; DP058507; DP058535; DP070216; DP070222; DP058572; DP058525]

Manchester and Salford show pockets of industrial development in Ancoats, particularly along the line of Shooter's Brook, where Messrs Salvin's factory and an ironworks were situated close to the bridge under Ancoats Lane (Great Ancoats Street) (Fig 4). A census of 1788 listed Thackeray's and Whitehead's Garratt Mill on the River Medlock to the south in 1783, and industrial expansion from the town centre towards Ancoats is shown by Peter Drinkwater's Piccadilly Mill of 1789; industrial colonies were also developing at New Islington at the end of Union (Redhill) Street, and at Holt Town, where David Holt established a water-powered factory in 1785.

Ancoats landowners began to realise the increasing value of their property. In 1775 part of the Great Croft between Ancoats Lane and Newton Lane (Oldham Road) was sold by the Leghs, a Cheshire gentry family, to Thomas Boond, a bricklayer, who sold off some of this two years later. Laurent's plan of Manchester and Salford (1793) (opposite) shows the area between Newton Lane and Union Street divided up on a gridiron pattern, less as town planning than to provide units of land attractive in terms of price or rent to small builders such as Thomas Boond. Land in these plots was sold and resold, often in small amounts, and houses, often of the back-to-back variety, together with domestic workshops, were erected upon it.

Rows of these houses faced onto streets named with reference to the original landowning families (George and Henry Cornwall Legh), to the developing trade of the area (Cotton, Silk) or to some rapidly departing rural ideal (Blossom, Primrose; Fig 5). Those sharing a common rear wall with them

Figure 6
A five-bay Georgian house, Oldham Street, photographed in 1959. With its three-bay central pediment and pedimented door-case, it would have been typical of the earliest developments in Ancoats.
[Manchester Archives and Local Studies m36564]

faced into enclosed courts bearing the names of lesser owners or landlords – Cleggs, Fieldings, Gerrards. This area, spreading eastwards from the junction of Ancoats Lane and Newton Lane at New Cross, was to provide problems for the socially concerned of later Victorian Manchester. Only the occasional building echoed the rather grander residential developments around Lever Street in the area to the west (Fig 6). At New Cross itself, the boundary between Manchester and Ancoats, an obelisk had been erected and neighbouring streets used for the sale of produce (Fig 7). The jumble of lanes around Gun Street and Henry Street still reflects the haphazard nature of this earliest development.

The boundaries of Ancoats were defined only when the Manchester and Salford Police Act of 1792 divided the towns into 14 police districts. Ancoats became Police District Number One, its boundaries being Newton Lane to the north, the River Medlock to the south and east, and Ancoats Lane to the west. It was the largest police district, 404 acres, and remained unchanged when

Manchester was incorporated in 1838. It became the New Cross Ward, which its elected councillors continued to represent until recently. A place with a population of more than 11,000 in 1801 had no recognition in local government nomenclature and no public buildings. Yet, in the first half of the 19th century it was to experience such rapid economic and demographic growth as to rival in population separate cotton towns such as Bolton or Oldham. A district where workers' homes mingled with industrial premises, large and small, it could claim to be the world's 'pioneer industrial suburb of the Industrial Revolution'. The detonators of that explosion of growth were canal building and steam-powered manufacturing.

Figure 7
By the early 19th century the commercial function of the area around New Cross, depicted in this painting c 1800, had become well established, with permanent market stalls and the Crown & Kettle public house. [Manchester Archives and Local Studies m03621]

3

Canals and factories

Canals were the arteries of Ancoats. They were the essential prerequisite to the area's industrial development: without them the construction of huge steam-powered, closely packed mills, which became the defining feature of the Ancoats townscape, would have been impossible. Two major waterways, the Ashton Canal and the Rochdale Canal, were to cross the area, with branches from them serving its major industrial sites (Fig 8). The construction of a canal from Manchester to Fairfield, with branches to Ashton-under-Lyne and to New Mill, near Oldham, was approved by Act of Parliament in 1792. Completed in 1799 and opened the following year, the Ashton Canal entered Manchester at Piccadilly, with cuts and basins along the western side of Ancoats Lane and across Pollard Street to serve adjacent factories (Fig 9). In 1794 another Act approved the plan to build a canal from Sowerby Bridge in Yorkshire via Hebden Bridge and Castleton near Rochdale to a Manchester terminus at Dale Street, where it would join the Ashton Canal (Fig 10).

Developing the canal system

By 1800 the Rochdale Canal was already constructed from the town to Ancoats Lane, where it terminated close to the first group of large Ancoats mills newly built by McConnel and Kennedy and by the Murray brothers. When the Rochdale Canal was finally completed in 1804, a cut through Manchester joined it and the Ashton Canal with the Castlefield basin of the earlier Bridgewater Canal. Further branches and basins served, for example, Brownsfield Mill and Jackson's Warehouse. By the first decade of the 19th century, west and east coasts of England were joined. The Rochdale Canal met the Calder and Hebble Canal at Sowerby Bridge, providing a waterway to the River Humber and the ports of Goole and Hull. The mills of Ancoats could import American raw cotton via Liverpool, coal from the collieries around Ashton, stone from Pennine quarries, and timber, via Hull, from the Baltic. This cut the cost of transporting such bulky materials by a quarter to a third of the price by road.

Royal Mill (McConnel's Old Mill, rebuilt 1912 and renamed 1942) in the foreground, and beyond it the eight-storey Sedgwick Mill of 1818–20, now the earliest surviving McConnel and Kennedy mill. When this 2008 photograph is compared to the 1820 image (Fig 12), Old Mill (1797) and Long Mill (1801–6) have gone, the former replaced by Royal Mill.
[DP068559]

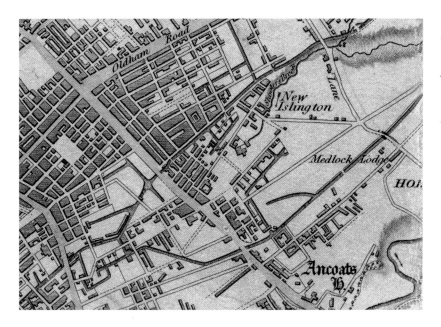

Figure 8
Ancoats in 1819. The contrasts with Laurent's map of
1793 (Fig 4) are striking. In the ensuing 26 years,
the Rochdale and Ashton canals have opened up Ancoats
for development and the Rochdale Canal is lined by mills.
Shooter's Brook, the former focus of industrial
developments, has largely been culverted.
[Detail from Johnson 1819. Courtesy of Digital
Archives Association]

Figure 9
The junction of the Rochdale and Ashton canals, north
of Dale Street. Small branches serving individual premises
proliferated; some of these survive, while the main lines
are still in use.
[NMR 20784/09]

The process of construction would have been well publicised in Manchester. The Rochdale Canal's promoters were forced to approach Parliament on three more occasions to raise another £313,000 in shares of £100 each, to add to the initial estimate of £291,000 which had proved to be far from adequate for the expense of land purchase and construction. The opening of the canal, on 21 December 1804, was celebrated by two boats, bearing the promoters and the band of the First Battalion of the Manchester and Salford Volunteers, sailing from Rochdale to Manchester. That evening another boat, laden with goods, completed the same voyage, and proceeded to Liverpool the next morning, proving the canal's economic worth. This trade from Rochdale westwards to Liverpool rivalled in importance the trans-Pennine trade. Even before this public display, sites close to both canals had become key ones for ambitious entrepreneurs, particularly those requiring regular supplies of bulky materials for building and subsequent manufacture, together with a safe and effective method of transporting finished goods to their point of sale.

In the first quarter of the 19th century, Ancoats witnessed a proliferation of branches off the Rochdale and Ashton canals to create a local network only rivalled in England by Birmingham's canal navigation system. It spread north-east along the Rochdale Canal and eastwards along the Ashton Canal from their junction at the Dale Street basin. This contributed to the distinctiveness of Ancoats by providing an arterial transport system for mills in the area, several decades before the coming of the railways (see Fig 8). Indeed, this canal network, and the very early intensive industrial and residential development it generated, is one of the distinguishing characteristics of Ancoats – unlike most industrial areas, railways are conspicuously absent from its core, with the mid-19th-century goods stations and rail-connected commodity markets relegated to its periphery.

An emerging mill-scape

With a developing market and transport system, conditions were ripe for an expansion of Manchester's burgeoning textile industry into the Ancoats area. Tentative at first, this expansion accelerated in the first decades of the 19th century to produce in Ancoats a remarkable landscape of intermingled mills, factories and housing that was to presage similar developments throughout the

Figure 10
A former lock-keeper's cottage. Spanning the entrance to a branch canal off the Ashton Canal, near Pollard Street, this is one of the few such canal buildings to survive to the late 20th century. Photographed in 1967, it has since been demolished.
[Manchester Archives and Local Studies m10465]

industrialising world. The massive steam-driven mills about to be erected in Ancoats were to become world-famous and the models for textile mills elsewhere.

Initially there was little to distinguish Ancoats from other parts of Manchester and surrounding towns. The first brick-built mills were relatively small scale and multi-purpose, sited to take advantage of what little water power there was. They scarcely rivalled the earlier large stone-built water-powered mills erected in the Derwent valley by Richard Arkwright at Cromford, and by his associates at Derby, Belper and Darley Abbey. The earliest Manchester mills were attracted to the River Medlock and its tributary Shooter's Brook. On the Medlock little survives of David Holt's cotton mill of 1785, yet this marked the beginnings of industrialisation in Ancoats, and by the 1790s an industrial colony at Holt Town had developed around Holt's Mill.

An examination of the property holdings of the sites depicted on William Green's 1794 *Plan of Manchester and Salford* confirms the typicality of the early development of Ancoats. It shows Newton Lane (Oldham Road) and adjacent lanes lined with weavers' cottages, and reveals that the Great Ancoats Street area had attracted associated trades such as fustian-cutters, hat-makers and machine-makers, while there was also a proliferation of flour dealers.

Shooter's Brook was the site of several water-powered textile mills and other small manufactories, including an ironworks and a pottery. Salvin's Factory of 1788 was followed by Shooter's Brook Mill and Ancoats Bridge Mill in the early 1790s, and by New Islington Mill in 1799. Nothing now survives above ground of these early mills, but recent archaeological work has revealed the significance of these sites for our understanding of the development of the textile industry. It has shown that attempts were being made by their owners to develop from inadequate water power to steam power, first by steam engines back-pumping water to augment the supply to water-wheels, then by erecting double-acting rotative steam engines to supply direct drive. These late 18th-century mill sites provide firm evidence of the evolutionary process of the harnessing of power that was to lead, in the decades bracketing the turn of the century, to the spectacular exploitation of steam power by an influx of talented immigrants.

In 1790 a Scottish engineer/machine-maker, Adam Murray, leased a plot of land on Union Street in Ancoats beside the line of the proposed Rochdale Canal. A few years later his example was followed by two more Scottish engineers, James McConnel and John Kennedy. These three, together with

Murray's brother George, who joined him in a partnership in 1798, were part of that wave of Scottish immigrants who contributed so much to England's industrial revolution. The sons of small farmers, or small-town shopkeepers in the Murrays' case, they all came from around the town of New Galloway in Kirkcudbright. Seeing little future for them on the Scottish borders, their parents sent them, when of suitable age, to be apprenticed to a machine-maker, William Cannan, an uncle of James McConnel, at Chowbent (Atherton), near Leigh, in industrialising Lancashire. Having completed their apprenticeships, they moved to Manchester to practise their trade, building cotton-spinning machinery in small workshops. Demand was high for the new spinning mule, so called because it combined the features of two earlier spinning machines, Hargreaves's spinning jenny and Arkwright's water-frame. Not only was it capable of producing superior yarn, but its inventor, Samuel Crompton of Bolton, had omitted to take out a patent on it. This made it free to use and to develop unhindered by patent rights.

The sale and repair of spinning machinery – particularly the mule to which Kennedy had made a number of improvements, including the direct use of steam power to drive it – generated significant profits (Fig 11). These,

Figure 11
John Kennedy's spinning mule.
[Reproduced from McConnel 1913]

in partnership with the Sandfords, warehouse owners, and a frugal lifestyle, provided the capital for the partnership of McConnel and Kennedy to build a large mill on Union Street, in 1797, at first leasing part of it for £370 a year. It was probably the first mill designed to contain powered spinning-mules, its scale, with 8 floors of 11 bays, each measuring 31 × 12m, dwarfing the nearby water-powered mills. It was powered by a 16hp Boulton and Watt steam engine, ordered in June 1797, which was housed in an external engine house and capable, by means of its rotary motion, of driving the machinery directly.

Four years later the partnership obtained more land to erect the eight-storey 'New Factory' with a larger (45hp) steam engine, placed in an internal engine house. Narrower than the original 'Old Mill', it became known as Long Mill. In 1817 the partnership bought a factory and some adjacent cottages from a Colonel Sedgwick to build another mill on Union Street, parallel to the Rochdale Canal (p 10). The watercolour of *c* 1820 shows the immense scale of the partnership's new mills – Long Mill was some 85m in length, and the complex's elevations to the Rochdale Canal totalled over 110m (Fig 12).

Figure 12
McConnel and Kennedy's mill, 1820.
[Manchester Archives and Local Studies m52533]

Similar complexes of large steam-driven textile mills were developing at this time elsewhere in Manchester, Leeds and even Shrewsbury, but nowhere rivalled the Ancoats area in concentration.

In 1798 the newly formed partnership of Adam and George Murray began to build an eight-storey mill on the land which Adam had leased in Union Street. This Union Mill or Old Mill was extended eastwards in 1801 to Bengal Street (Figs 13 and 14). In 1804 another mill, New Mill, was erected on Jersey Street. By 1805 wings had been built along Bengal Street and Murray Street for warehousing or office purposes. These linked Old and Decker mills with New Mill, completing a quadrangle of buildings with a street entrance on Murray Street (Fig 15). The construction of the Scottish entrepreneurs' first mills coincided with the opening of the Rochdale Canal. The Murrays' mill complex had a canal basin at its centre, with access to the canal by a tunnel under Union Street. In their early days McConnel and Kennedy relied more on road transport, a strictly worded contract with a new firm, Pickfords, providing for the regular transport of coal and raw cotton to the mill, and of cotton yarn from it.

Both firms used Boulton and Watt steam engines with their rotary motion to drive the machinery (Fig 16). More powerful engines and larger mules were installed as profits accrued and more advanced engines became available. The spinning machinery, requiring a great deal of space, operated on the upper floors of the new factories, with carding and other preparatory processes being carried out on the lower floors and the cleaning of raw cotton in segregated areas. By 1809 McConnel and Kennedy were using another new technical development, gas lighting, which the Murrays adopted later, around 1819. This enabled work to begin in the early morning and continue into the evening during the dark winter months. Seasonal restrictions on work were lifted.

In their origins McConnel, Kennedy and the Murray brothers were typical of the new entrepreneurs of Britain's industrial revolution. Ambitious, frugal and probably ruthless, they were able to amass very quickly the capital required to build and operate such large factories. The engineering skills they had learned during their apprenticeships and early business careers were central to their success. Not only were early profits made from machine sales, but they were able to build, repair and improve the machinery required for their own enterprises. Machinery was perhaps the most expensive capital input for a would-be cotton master. Space could be hired, at least initially, while labour, especially of the unskilled or semi-skilled variety, was cheap, and able to provide its own housing. Demand in a period of war and inflation, such as the first decade of the 19th century, was high for the very fine yarn which the two firms produced and sold initially through contacts in the Glasgow market.

With a mixture of good management and good luck, these Scottish partnerships rapidly outstripped their rivals to become untypical of the industry. A survey of 1811 by Samuel Crompton, the inventor of the spinning mule, showed McConnel and Kennedy operating 84,000 spindles on their

Figure 13
Survivals of the Murrays' early buildings, including Old Mill (1798) and Decker Mill (1801–2). Most of the mill ranges and engine houses around the canal basin date from before 1817; a major loss to fire was the Bengal Street block of 1805. To the east on the other side of Bengal Street the New Little Mill of 1909 and the adjacent Fireproof and Doubling Mills are later rebuilds.
[NMR 20785/54]

McConnel & Kennedy's mills
 1 Royal Mill
 2 Sedgwick Mill
   (a) West wing
   (b) East wing
   (c) North block
 3 Sedgwick New Mill
 4 Paragon Mill

A & G Murray's mills
 5 Old Mill
 6 Decker Mill
 7 Murray Street Block
 8 Murrays' New Mill
 9 New Little Mill
 10 Doubling Mill
 11 Fireproof Mill
 12 Beehive Mill

Figure 14
Murrays' Mills at their early peak, depicted in a print that has become a classic image of the Industrial Revolution. The three-storey 18th-century factory building in the foreground, belonging to a Mr Lane, pre-dates the canal, and was occupied by Adam Murray in the early 19th century. It provides a vivid contrast with the massive mills behind.
[Austin and Gahey 1835. Manchester Archives and Local Studies m52534]

Figure 15
A gated archway from Murray Street. This controlled access to an enclosed courtyard at Murrays' Mills with its canal basin. Inside the entrance, mounted on the wall for safekeeping and inscribed with a Victorian tribute, is a part of the former tomb of Adam Murray, one of the founding brothers of the mill complex.
[DP058615]

mules, and the Murrays, 85,000. The great majority of Manchester spinning firms operated fewer than 10,000 each. With more than 1,000 employees each by 1816, the two firms far outstripped the average Manchester spinning enterprise with 300. The huge buildings on Union Street soon became one of the sights of Manchester to which visitors were directed. A German visitor, Peter Beuth, wrote in 1823 to the architect Karl Friedrich Schinkel:

> It is only here, my friend, that the machinery and buildings can be found commensurate with the miracles of modern times – they are called factories. Such a barn of a place is eight or nine storeys high, up to forty windows long and usually four windows deep ... in addition a forest of steam engine chimneys, so like needles that one cannot comprehend how they stay up, present a wonderful sight from a distance, especially at night when the thousands of windows are brightly illuminated with gas light.

Schinkel, visiting three years later, appeared to be less impressed. 'It makes a dreadful and dismal impression,' he wrote, 'monstrous shapeless buildings put up only by foremen without architecture, only the least that was necessary

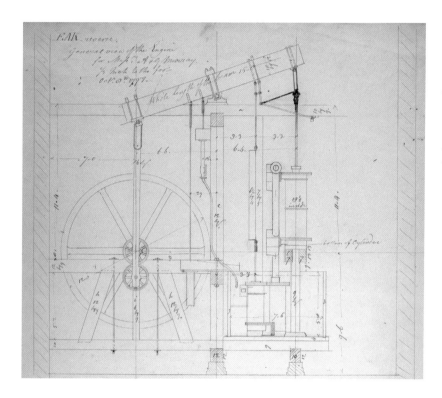

Figure 16
Boulton & Watt design drawing of an engine for A & G
Murray, 1798. James Watt's rotary steam engines
overcame the dependence of mills on water power and
enabled manufacturers, such as the Murrays, to site their
factories in towns close to transport, warehousing and
labour without the need for water, except for that
required by the steam engine boiler and condenser.
This could be supplied from a canal.
[Reproduced with the permission of Birmingham
Libraries & Archives, Boulton & Watt Collection,
Birmingham Library]

and out of red brick' (Fig 17). Another German, the young Friedrich Engels,
visiting in 1842, noted that 'in the last mentioned broad district, included under
the name Ancoats, stand the largest mills of Manchester, lining the canals,
colossal six and seven storied buildings towering with their slender chimneys
far above the low cottages of the workers.'

Though dominant, McConnel and Kennedy and the Murrays were far from
having a monopoly of cotton spinning in Ancoats, although they produced the
finest yarn, the 'highest counts', measured by the number of hanks of finished
yarn, each 840 yards long, made from one pound of cotton. Firms such as
Pollards (Fig 18), B & W Sandford and Gallimore & Johnson were presences
in the Ancoats industry, some for a time combining the processes of machine
spinning and power-loom weaving. Some mills, such as the Brownsfield (Fig 19)
or the Beehive (Figs 20 and 21), operated on the 'room and power' principle.

Figure 17
Schinkel's sketch of Union Street mills, 1826.
[Reproduced, with permission, from The English
Journey *1993, 177]*

Figure 18
Jonathan Pollard's immense cotton twist mill
(demolished) on Great Ancoats Street, beside the Ashton
Canal. In 1809 J Simpson owned the third largest mill.
The Murrays, the Kennedys and the other Scottish
entrepreneurs were not the only presences in Ancoats.
[J F Harris 1825. Mr Pollard's Cotton Twist Mill.
Manchester Archives and Local Studies m52452]

Figure 19
Brownsfield Mill, built, in 1825, of slow-burning wood construction. It fronts the Rochdale Canal but was originally served by a branch canal. Its engine house in the southern gable, which would have contained a tall beam engine, is clearly distinguished by the differences in fenestration.
[DP058527]

Figure 20
Beehive Mill, Radium Street, a room-and-power mill with an internal engine house. The main range was built by the early 1820s and is of slow-burning wood construction, while the three-bay extension of 1824 on Jersey Street is of fireproof construction.
[DP068549]

Figure 21 (opposite)
The attic of Beehive Mill, with its distinctive curved cast-iron roof trusses. It was also powered to allow it to be rented. This restored attic of the main block now provides a fine space for events.
[DP058523]

A new entrant to the industry could rent part of the mill, draw power from its steam engine to run his machinery and hope to make profits on which expansion could take place. Other trades, such as weaving or the cutting of fustian, a cheap, hard-wearing twilled cloth with a linen warp and a cotton weft, were carried out in small workshops or in the homes of the producers (Fig 22). Handloom weaving died a slow and agonising death as the factory-based power loom became more effective from the 1820s.

Figure 22
Spinning and weaving in an attic room.
[H E Tidmarsh 1894. The Age of Industry: Spinning and Hand Loom Weaving. *© Manchester City Galleries (1894.10)]*

Maturing mills and diversifying industries

The frenetic period of mill building initiated by the close-knit Scottish families only gradually slowed down in the second quarter of the 19th century, as the first generation of owners passed away. It had already seen spectacular growth:

when Adam Murray died in 1818, at the age of 52, the family firm was worth nearly three times its 1809 value, but his brother George, as sole partner, continued the expansion by building further mills in the adjacent block of land to the east. Thus by the middle of the century, when George Murray at the age of 93 relinquished his role of managing director (a year before his death), these new mills – Little Mill and Doubling Mill, which were linked to the earlier quadrangle by underground passages – had very appreciably increased the size of the factory. Similarly, when John Kennedy retired in 1826, McConnel appointed his two eldest sons as partners: the firm traded as McConnel & Co and continued to expand and modernise, first with structural modifications within the existing buildings by the local engineers William Fairbairn and James Lillie, then in 1868 by a large new extension to Sedgwick Mill by A H Stott, who was to become one of the most noted mill architects of his generation.

The plans published in 1851 by Joseph Adshead of the New Cross Ward (surveyed 1850) give an idea of the extent of these two developments and of the many other cotton mills in the wider area of Ancoats served by the Rochdale and Ashton canals (Figs 23 and 24), and put names to many of these mills. Thus, for example, to the west and north of the Rochdale Canal we find Jersey Street Mill, with Purnell and Thompson's Mill to the east, Armitage & Wards and Faulkners Mills in Rodney Street, Bodgshaw & Nephews Mill off Elizabeth Street, and Lloyd Field Cotton Mills and J Chadwick's Brook Mill on Lloyd Street. Between the Rochdale Canal and the Ashton Canal there are a further six cotton mills and associated dye-works and warp-sizing works. By this time Shooter's Brook – the original focus of mills in the area – had largely disappeared underground, with a short section reappearing at an old cotton mill being used as a temporary 'Fever Ward'.

As these plans show, cotton was not Ancoats' only industry. Engineering was central to the development of the cotton industry. McConnel, Kennedy and the Murray brothers were machine-makers whose skill was essential to their development as cotton spinners. The illustrious 19th-century engineer William Fairbairn describes in his autobiography how, as a struggling entrant to the trade in 1817, he was given a contract by George Murray to renew horizontal cross-shafts at Murrays' Mills. Working from five in the morning to nine at night, he improved the machinery, much to Murray's delight. As a result, he was recommended to McConnel and Kennedy to design and erect the

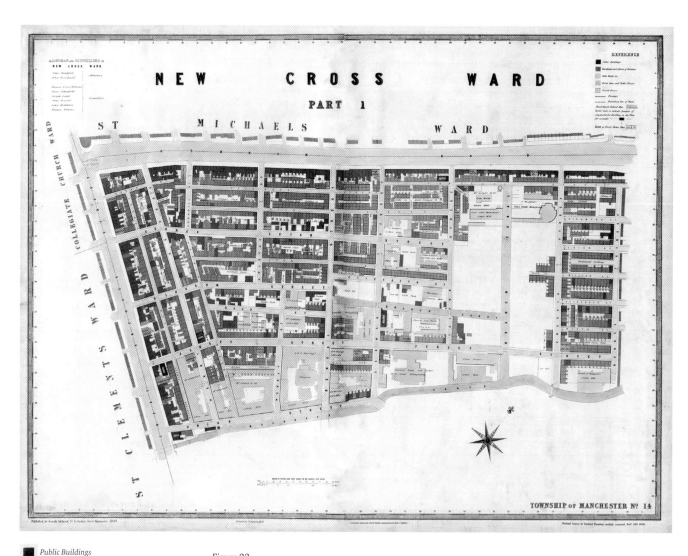

Public Buildings

Warehouses and places of Business

Mills, Works &c

Hotels, Inns, and Public Houses

Private Houses

Figure 23
New Cross Ward, Part 1. Adshead's plans are a mine of information, differentiating between dwellings and industrial, commercial and institutional buildings. In this area of Ancoats the density of the housing, the textile mills by the canals and the numerous public houses are tellingly illustrated.
[Adshead 1851 No. 14. Courtesy of Digital Archives Association]

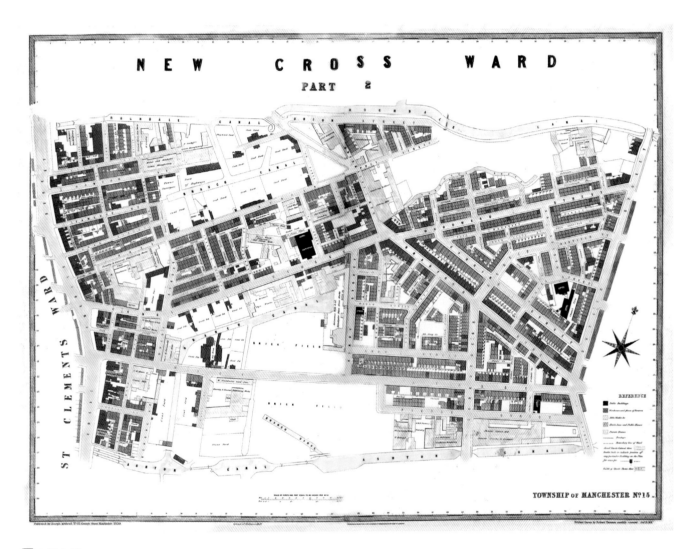

Public Buildings

Warehouses and places of Business

Mills, Works &c

Hotels, Inns, and Public Houses

Private Houses

Figure 24
New Cross Ward, Part 2. The area bracketed by the Rochdale and Ashton canals has more diversity of industry and social provision. Iron foundries, warehouses and other works are interspersed with the textile mills, while several chapels and schools are shown.
[Adshead 1851 No. 15. Courtesy of Digital Archives Association]

machinery at the new Sedgwick Mill. By 1850 the firm of Fairbairn & Co occupied several separate premises in the area between the two main canals, with its main works, machine works and offices on Canal Street, and a large site to the south served by a branch off the Ashton Canal (Fig 25).

A similar mix of industrial premises was sited between the Ashton Canal and the River Medlock – a further eight cotton mills, a silk mill, dye-works, Swindells & Williams's large chemical works and Peel & Williams's Soho Foundry. The last named, established between the canal and Pollard Street around 1810, manufactured components for steam engines and boilers, and later specialised in the manufacture of gear wheels (Fig 26). Numerous small businesses such as iron stores and screw and bolt works supplied other Ancoats engineers, for example John Hetherington at the Vulcan Works and Samuel Bowler's foundry.

Glass-making was another prominent Ancoats industry. As early as 1785 Imison and King established a 'glass house' on Newton Lane. Although this was short-lived, the 19th century saw a concentration of the industry in Ancoats,

Figure 25
Fairbairn's mechanical engineering works, Canal Street. The dense mix of foundries, engineering works and mills shown here was the subject of remark even in the mid-19th century.
[H Milligan 1853. Manchester Archives and Local Studies m61065]

Figure 26
An engraving of Peel & Williams's Soho Foundry yard,
situated on the Ashton Canal. The range of mechanical
goods laid out illustrates the firm's concentration on
mill work.
[Thomas Slack 1814. Manchester Archives and Local
Studies m61384]

and by its heyday in the last quarter of the century there were nine glass-works in production throughout the district. Some of these started quite early in the century: the Stourbridge Flint Glass Works opened in 1831 off Oldham Street, while the Manchester Flint Glass Works in Canal Street started in 1827. Percival Vickers, one of the most famous of these enterprises, opened its British & Foreign Flint Glass Works on Jersey Street in 1844 (Fig 27), and by mid-century it and other firms – such as Molineaux, Webb & Co (1827–1936) of Kirby Street and Burtles, Tate & Co of Poland Street – were producing large quantities of bowls, jugs and carafes for Victorian tables (Fig 28).

Much of the output was for mass consumption and typically consisted of items made of press-moulded glass, using technology invented in the United States in 1825. However, leading firms such as Molineaux, Webb & Co also employed a variety of techniques to produce high-quality artistic glassware, and even exhibited at the Great Exhibition in 1851. In the 'Industry of All Nations' section of the exhibition catalogue appears the comment that 'one is apt to associate the manufacturing productions of Manchester with cotton and calicoes', and surprise is expressed at seeing 'an exhibition of beautiful GLASS-WORK emanating from that busy town ... it is not generally known that not less than twenty-five tons of flint-glass are ... produced weekly in Manchester'.

The industry contracted greatly in the first quarter of the 20th century but lingered on until it ceased in 1959. In a period of over a century Ancoats had produced much of Manchester's glass, from elaborate swan-shaped vases to

Figure 27
An engraving of the Percival Vickers glass works on Jersey Street.
[© Ian Miller. Reproduced, with permission, from the cover of Percival Vickers 1902 catalogue Glass Shades for Electric Lights, Cut and Moulded*]*

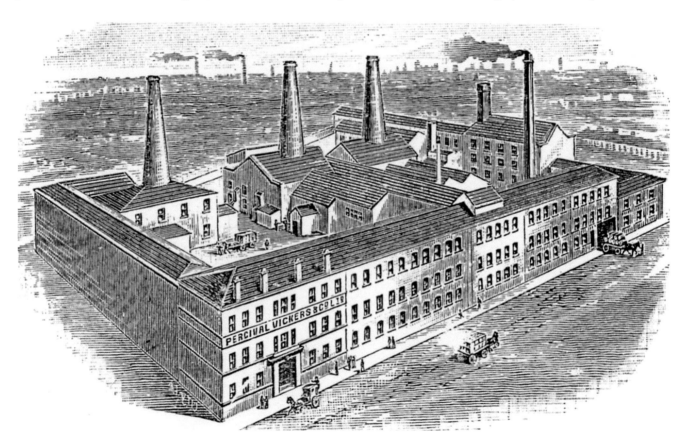

more humble jugs and bottles, as well as a huge range of the industrial glassware required by chemical firms and others (Fig 29). 'They lived their lives in dust,' Bart Kennedy wrote of the glass cutters in 1905:

> glass-dust, sand-dust and dust of pumice-stone. All the day they stood at their troughs, grinding and cutting and smoothing and polishing glassware on the swift-running wheels. In the early morning and the evening when the lights were lit the patting shop made a strange picture. Here were pale-faced men deftly holding and turning and twisting beautiful shining objects of glass. Swift-turning wheels, brilliant, shining glass, and pale, intent men. And the sound, at once dull and piercing, of grinding and cutting. A scene squalid and picturesque.

These many industries were served by numerous small stores and warehouses, while extensive coal-, timber- and stone-yards lined the branches off the main canals. Indeed, timber-yards, importing from the Baltic via the Rochdale Canal, were a prominent aspect of Ancoats' industrial geography, spawning small workshops and domestic industries making furniture, floorboards and picture frames. Service industries, builders, joiners, glaziers and plumbers set up shop wherever space was available, as did wheelwrights, farriers and blacksmiths servicing the horse-dependent transport industries. Iron and brass foundries added their noise and smoke to what had become by mid-century a densely packed industrial suburb with a population of more than 50,000.

Figure 28 (above)
Decanter, manufactured by Molineaux, Webb & Co,
c 1865–70.
[© Manchester City Galleries 1977.5]

Figure 29 (left)
Vase and flower holder moulded into the shape of a swan,
manufactured by Burtles, Tate & Co, c 1885. Opalescent
pressed glass.
[© Manchester City Galleries 1984.75]

'No more injurious and demoralising method of housing the workers has yet been discovered'

Friedrich Engels, *The Condition of the Working Class in England*, 1845

4

The pioneer suburb and its workers

Primrose Street, c 1895. A condemned terrace showing dwellings with workshops above and warehousing. [Photo: W H Farrow. Manchester Archives and Local Studies m10502]

The rapid growth of industries in Ancoats from the 1780s made it a magnet for those seeking jobs both in construction and in manufacturing. In the Police District Number One a population of 11,000 at the first national census of 1801 grew to 31,000 by 1831 and reached a peak of 56,000 in 1861. Indeed if Ancoats had been a town in its own right it would have ranked in the top 40 towns in England. However, the 1850 Adshead survey reveals its urban shortcomings – a comparative lack of religious or municipal institutions and amenities. Many of the immigrants came from rural settlements in the surrounding counties of Lancashire, Cheshire and Derbyshire, some having skills of spinning or weaving learned in domestic industry. A large number, however, were Irish immigrants attracted by tales of work and wages in north-west England. In 1832, well before the Irish potato famine of the 1840s with its terrible aftermath, Dr James Kay, physician to the Ancoats and Ardwick Dispensary, wrote: 'the Newtown and Ancoats Districts have always contained a greater proportion of Irish than any other portion of town'. By the mid-century their numbers were to swell greatly, driven from their homeland by famine and expulsion from the land. In 1851, 46 per cent of adult men in Ancoats were recorded in the census as Irish-born, as were both husband and wife in 45 per cent of married couples in the district.

A recent study by Lee Gregory examined the demographic detail of the residents across an area of streets in central Ancoats and analysed the origins of heads of household, the occupational structure and the occupancy rates. Its findings confirmed the overwhelming preponderance of Irish-born inhabitants in the early and mid-19th century and their initial correlation with poorer housing, with higher rates of occupancy per dwelling and with employment in the textile industry. Initially these families tended to live in close communities such as Gerrards Court, a block of 45 back-to-back houses off Bengal Street, 58 per cent of which, the 1851 census indicates, was occupied by Irish heads of household. It also appears from contemporary accounts that these ghetto-like communities of Irish migrant workers were regarded with some hostility by the local Mancunian population.

Employment, conditions and the workplace

The new system of factory production using steam-powered machinery was a major source of attraction. The huge mills of the Murray brothers and of McConnel and Kennedy on Union Street were employing some 1,500 workers each by 1830. These, of course, were exceptional in their size. More typical were factories employing a few hundred operatives; some of the small producers in 'room and power mills' employed under 100 workers. Women and children supplied the majority of a textile factory's workforce (Fig 30). Men were employed either for their experience and skill as overlookers, mechanics and

Figure 30
A scene, in a textile mill, illustrating the division of labour between men, women and children.
[From Baines 1835. Manchester Archives and Local Studies m59219]

mule spinners, or for physical strength in unloading raw cotton and coal, loading spun cotton yarn or stoking the furnaces of the steam engines. Women tended the machinery under the supervision of a male mule-spinner, aided by children performing such tasks as sweeping up waste cotton (scavengers) and cleaning machinery, their size being convenient for crawling under the spinning mules ranged across the mill floor. Door handles in parts of Murrays' Mills are set low, doubtless to allow children ease of access (Fig 31).

Work began at six or seven in the morning and continued, with the aid of gas lighting, into the early evening. Mill spinning rooms were kept hot and damp to prevent cotton threads breaking, and their air was heavy with dust. Operatives usually worked barefoot on the oil-soaked floors, and lightly clad: women in shifts, men and boys in shirt and trousers, with clogs – and for women, shawls – ready to be put on before venturing out into the Ancoats air. George Murray, giving evidence to a Commission of Inquiry in 1834, claimed that rooms in his mill were kept at a temperature of about 75°F, but that there was a casement in every window so that workers could control the ventilation. A closet was situated in every room, and buckets of water were provided for washing. A half-hour break was given for breakfast and an hour at dinner time, when workers could choose whether to go home or eat their food in the factory. No child under 9 was employed; for those aged 9 to 13, their daily hours of work were limited to 11½ for a six-day week. Unruly children were admonished or dismissed, corporal punishment being disapproved of. Since most children were employed by the operatives themselves, however, it was not possible to prevent some physical chastisement of children.

Child labour in textile factories had become a subject of national concern in the early 19th century. The Factory Act of 1833 forbade the employment of children under 9, and limited the hours of those aged 9 to 13 and of 'young persons' between 13 and 18 years. Some 11 years later another Act further limited child labour, leading some employers to use groups of children in relays so that adult workers would always have youngsters on the mill floor to perform menial tasks. Murray, though complying with the new regulation, insisted that child workers were essential to his business and that parents could find no better employment for their children than in cotton mills.

Wages for cotton factory work varied. Most employees were paid piece rates, and had to pay their young assistants out of their own earnings. A male

Figure 31
Murrays' Old Mill, 1798. The low height at which the handle to the courtyard door is set is evidence of the essential role of children in early 19th-century mill operation.
[DP070293]

mule spinner in a fine-yarn spinning mill such as Murrays or McConnel & Kennedy's might earn 50 to 60s at top rate, although 20 or 25s was more likely in smaller mills producing coarser yarns. Female piecers were cheaper at 10 to 12s a week, with child workers being paid 6 or 7s. Family earnings, if husband, wife and older children were employed, might compare favourably with those outside the area; female and child earnings were essential to the support of Ancoats families. Cotton mill work was relatively secure, although trade depressions, strikes or the not unlikely disaster of a mill fire could affect earnings severely. For all George Murray's confidence, labour turnover was high – 42 per cent of his workforce in 1819 left after less than a year's employment. Labour in Ancoats was young and highly volatile.

Sections of the local textile industry still operated on the domestic system. St George's parish marriage and baptismal records show more fathers occupied as hand weavers than as factory workers in the 1820s, although the trade was already threatened by the power loom. The cutting of fustian, sewing and tailoring, carried out in the home or in small, upper-storey workshops, survived, particularly as an occupation for women who shunned the alternative of domestic service to a greater degree than in other parts of Manchester. Earnings ranged between 9 and 15s a week, while less fortunate women had to exist on the few shillings a week earned by sewing shirts or taking in washing.

Employment opportunities were by no means confined to the cotton industry. The greater Ancoats area was the location of a wide range of trades and industries, hence its attraction for those seeking work. Adult males, a minority in cotton spinning, found work in textile finishing trades such as bleaching, dyeing and fustian cutting. Many more were employed in the numerous glass works, the engineering works and foundries, and the timber-yards. The building trades alone employed some 20 per cent of adult males in Ancoats in 1851, probably more during the hectic period of construction between the 1790s and the 1830s. Labouring jobs at canal wharves and warehouses, building sites and workshops attracted unskilled males, particularly Irish immigrants, over 80 per cent of whom were employed at these tasks in 1851, with earnings of 3 to 4s a week.

Small workshops, cheek by jowl with houses, produced furniture, picture frames, umbrellas, bonnets and gas burners. Woodturners made spindles for

Figure 32
Wooden and metal spinning components found at Murrays' Mills whilst it was being restored. [Courtesy of Heritage Works/BDP]

Figure 33
Men, photographed in front of a 'Labor Home', collecting and chopping wood as a condition of their night's stay at Jactin House (see p 47).
[c 1893. Manchester Archives and Local Studies m68452]

the spinning mills, or hat blocks for the hatters of Stockport (Fig 32). The development by Manchester Corporation of the large Smithfield Market on nearby Swan Street provided jobs for men in labouring and portering, and for both sexes in hawking and stall holding on the market's fringes (Fig 33). In 1865 Henry Oats of the Manchester Statistical Society found, to his intense disgust, that hawkers in Ancoats, 'of whom there is a large number living in the district', kept their draught animals, ponies and donkeys, in the kitchens of their tiny houses. In the industrial suburb, work and domestic life were inextricably mixed.

Housing the workers

As well as finding work, the newcomer to Ancoats had to find somewhere to live. Given a large and growing pool of labour, few employers had any need to provide housing for their workforce except perhaps to retain a highly skilled artisan or a trusted person to carry out janitorial duties. James McConnel possessed 18 houses in Maria Street in 1829, and George Murray, 15 in Gas Street. Only four of their tenants, however, were described as cotton spinners, and Murray told the inquiry of 1834 that few of his workers lived in houses provided by the company. Millworkers and others had to find their own housing as close to their place of work as possible given the absence of any affordable means of public transport.

From the 1790s, houses sprang up rapidly on the small, rectangular blocks of land into which the district was divided. The first, dating from the 1780s or 1790s, were built in the angle formed by Great Ancoats Street and Oldham Road, spreading north-eastwards towards German (now Radium) Street and Union (now Redhill) Street. These small parcels of building land were let and sublet, rapidly losing any contact with their original owners, such as the Leigh family, except for the payment of chief rent and the occasional street name. Sub-lessees – mostly small businessmen, publicans, pawnbrokers or members of the building trade such as stone masons, plumbers or glaziers – ran up as many houses as possible on the land available to them, hoping to gain enough from rents to compensate them and provide for widows and children before leases fell in or the houses fell down.

Figure 34 (left)
Ancoats as seen from the roof of Victoria Hall, c 1897. Residential and industrial properties are in close proximity and smoke from their chimneys intermingles. [Manchester Archives and Local Studies m09992]

Figure 35 (below, left)
Nos 13 and 15 Blossom Street, 1903. Manchester was notorious for its cellar dwellings, which were often accessed separately with no communication with the houses above. [Photo: A Bradburn. Manchester Archives and Local Studies m11033]

Figure 36 (below)
Poland Street, 1897. This photograph shows the essence of late 19th-century Ancoats – a mix of houses and commercial properties letting directly onto gas-lit cobbled streets. [Photo: H Entwistle. Manchester Archives and Local Studies m10401]

The very worst of this housing has long since gone – condemned in the mid-19th century – but illustrations reproduced here from the later clearances still convey an impression of the narrow cobbled streets with their tight mix of industrial and residential properties, and of the meanness of much of the housing (Fig 34). The images of Primrose, Blossom, Poland, Sherratt, Gun and Rodney streets show a variety of two- and three storey brick-built terraced houses, some with and some without basements, close built to the roads, and interspersed with small industrial premises and public houses. The diversity of detail and use bears testimony to constant change within the piecemeal development process that was to typify Ancoats (p 32, Figs 35 and 36).

Diversity and change

Despite its intensity the process of development from rural fringe to urban housing was by no means uniform. Within the dense urban landscape was a rich tapestry of constantly changing detail. In-depth study of an area of two blocks at the heart of Ancoats sheds light on the general picture. These blocks, centred on Loom Street and bordered by Spittal, George Leigh, Bengal and Blossom streets, encapsulate many of the changes in urban housing over a period of two centuries that was to typify Ancoats. The development of the area is first recorded on Laurent's 1793 topographical plan (*see* Fig 4) and Green's 1794 plan of Manchester and Salford. These depict terraces of small houses along Loom Street and larger properties at the corners of Bengal Street and George Leigh Street which, according to late 18th-century directories, were occupied by machine-makers and flour dealers. The presence of these larger properties is an indication that Ancoats, being a relatively open rural area at this time, was a quite desirable place to live, and indeed mill owners such as the Murray brothers and John Kennedy initially had houses on the two main roads bordering the area. In this respect it resembled the outskirts of other industrial towns which were to experience similar change from predominantly residential to a densely developed mix of industrial premises and workers' housing – the emerging Birmingham Jewellery Quarter north of St Paul's Square is the best contemporary example, where back-to-backs and courts of workers' houses are intermingled with factories and converted villas surrounded by workshops.

Some 25 years later Johnson's map of 1819 (*see* Fig 8) shows that, despite the penetration of the area by the Rochdale Canal with its branch to Bengal Street, and the huge mill complexes lining the canal, there were still significant open spaces at the heart of Ancoats. The Loom Street area itself, however, was already being built up with further properties, and Bancks & Co's 1832 *Plan of Manchester and Salford, with their Environs* confirms that this infill was back-to-back and side-back housing. These brick-built types of housing, of the meanest construction, with small rooms and minimal facilities, were already becoming synonymous with urban squalor. Many such houses were two-storey dwellings,

BACK to BACK HOUSES.

Figure 37
Back-to-back houses illustrated from an aerial perspective, c 1850.
[Manchester Archives and Local Studies m08386]

one room deep, and built back to back, their rooms 7ft (2.13m) high and perhaps 12 × 14ft (3.65 × 4.26m) square. One row faced onto the street, the other, with which it shared a common rear wall, faced into a court, reached by a passage or ginnel from the street (Figs 37 and 38). These courts might contain one or two ash privies and a water pump or tap. Jepson's Court and Blossom Court in the Loom Street area were among the many examples of these, while the names of the nearby Clegg's Yard, Fielding's Yard or Bennett's Court perhaps give a clue as to the builders or landlords.

Some of the larger houses were three or four storeys high, with the uppermost storey often being used as a workshop. Many had cellars beneath them. Several families might occupy such houses, one family to a room, with

Figure 38
Condemned back-to-back houses were replaced with dwellings such as the terraced housing shown in this 2008 aerial photograph.
[Detail from NMR 20786/18]

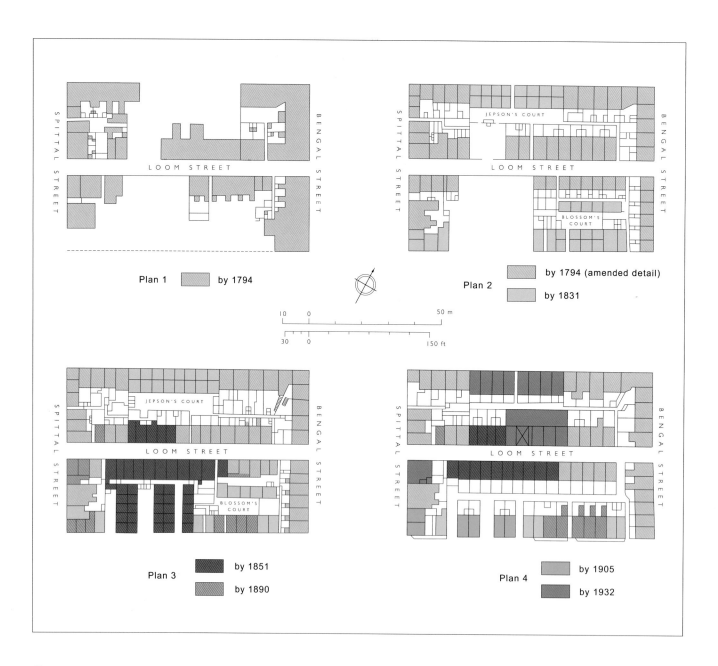

another, or perhaps a single person, in the cellar. Rents varied but probably averaged, by mid-century, around 3s a week, with a cellar, dark and damp, to be had for as little as 6d. Overcrowding was rife. Oats's 1865 survey found 19 per cent of families in this part of Ancoats living in one room, husband, wife and children perhaps sharing space with a lodger. Ash closet privies were often shared by several families, with ginnels and empty houses sometimes being used for toilet purposes. In one case 12 families used the same privy, which was locked by the keyholder at 10 o'clock every evening. Social investigators focused, of course, on the worst examples in order to make the case for sanitary reform. These appalling living conditions were mirrored in many other industrial towns and cities – London's 'rookeries' were notorious, as were the 'yards' in Leeds and the 'courts' in Birmingham. Leeds passed an Improvement Act in 1866 stipulating that back-to-back houses had to be built in terraces no more than four pairs long, while Birmingham banned construction of new back-to-backs in 1876. However, conditions were such in Manchester that the town council had to act much earlier. It passed a byelaw banning further building of back-to-backs in 1844, and the leasing of cellar dwellings in 1853, with most being closed by 1868. By the 1840s most streets in Ancoats were paved, and drained with nearly 30 miles of sewer.

For the Loom Street area these measures arrived rather late, as the first large-scale Ordnance Survey map surveyed in 1848 shows that by that date the entire two blocks had already been densely developed with back-to-back housing. The regulations did, however, have a beneficial effect. Succeeding maps, such as Adshead's of 1851 and the OS 1:2500 map of 1888, show a gradual decrease in the number of back-to-backs, first by the expediency of removing the one-brick-thick party walls to provide 'through houses', and then by selective demolition and the extra provision of backyards and privies (Fig 39). Thus by 1905 the worst of the back-to-back courts off Blossom Street had been demolished or converted. Those of Jepsom's Court fronting George Leigh Street survived into the 20th century, when they were finally converted into through houses. The OS 1:2500 map of 1932 shows the cumulative effect of these improvements but also shows the first replacement of houses by a commercial property – a warehouse in Loom Street. Post-war maps record the gradual eradication of all houses in the area, a process that was complete by the end of the century.

Figure 39
Phased plans, centred on Loom Street, demonstrating the development of housing. They chart the introduction, and eventual disappearance, of back-to-back and court dwellings.
[Plan 1 based on Green 1787–94; Plan 2, on Johnson 1819 and Bancks 1832; Plan 3, on OS 1:10 560 map 1851, Adshead 1851 and OS 1:2 500 map 1888; Plan 4, on OS 1:2 500 maps 1905 and 1932]

Later house building, as it spread northwards and eastwards, was of rather better quality. Friedrich Engels, writing in 1845 of the area he had visited with one of its residents, the millworker Mary Burns, found that, in the newly built streets, 'the cottages look neat and cleanly, doors and windows are new and freshly painted, the rooms within newly whitewashed'. He noted, however, that even these apparently 'neat and substantial cottages' were shoddily built, their owners unlikely to spend money on repairs to avoid 'diminishing their rent receipts'. Engels attributed the thin walls to speculative builders, under

Figure 40
Excavations of Loom Street housing by the University of Manchester Archaeological Unit, 2007. These have verified the meanness of construction commented on by Engels in 1845 – many of the walls are only one brick thick.
[© Ian Miller]

conditions of the leasehold property rights, maximising rentable space in the minimum of area and expense.

The surprising variation of housing types, and Engels's comments about the meanness of construction, have recently been verified. During the summer of 2007 the University of Manchester Archaeological Unit undertook a series of excavations in the now cleared two blocks of the Loom Street area in advance of redevelopment. The excavation areas were targeted to investigate differences in layout and standards of construction between the various housing types of different periods, and to ascertain the provision of features such as cellars, backyards and sanitary facilities. The excavations did indeed substantiate many of the alleged differences – the early housing on the Bengal Street corner was grander in construction, detail, layout and provision of services than that of contemporary houses in Loom Street and later housing throughout the area. The thick party walls and an impressive column base and fine pediment mount hinted at a fine house with a substantial doorway, while the deep cellars and yards were well paved. The latter contained privies and a well-appointed drainage system. In contrast the excavations of areas of later meaner housing revealed poor construction with single-brick-thick party walls, small living spaces and ill-drained inhabited cellars, while in some instances even the gable walls were only one brick thick, verifying Engels's observations (Fig 40). Angus Reach, reporting on the workers of Manchester for the *Morning Chronicle* in 1849, found a better class of housing to the south of the town in Hulme as compared with the 'older, worse built and in all respects inferior quarter of Ancoats'. Even the furnishing of Ancoats homes appeared to him to be of inferior quality: 'a very fair proportion of what was deal in Ancoats was mahogany in Hulme'.

Overcrowding of Ancoats houses eased after 1870, with a declining population, partly the result of the movement of more affluent workers outwards to more purely residential suburbs, their journeys to work aided by the development of the tramway system. Fewer families took in lodgers, giving them more living space. In a less vibrant housing market, however, there existed few incentives to small landlords to improve their properties. By the end of the 19th century, much of Ancoats housing was a century old and in a poor state of repair. Housing in the pioneer industrial suburb suffered from its early start. Succeeding chapters will relate the measures, some drastic, taken to ameliorate the problem.

5

The architecture of social concern

The population of the greater Ancoats area reached a peak of 56,000 in 1861. After that, numbers declined to 46,000 by 1891. It remained a wholly working-class community, much of it, by later in the century, belonging to a pool of casual labourers and small traders living a hand-to-mouth existence in crowded and deteriorating housing. The hostility that originally greeted the Irish immigrant ghettos of the early 19th century lessened with the spread of Irish inhabitants to a better standard of housing in the district. Though they retained their sense of communal identity, their assimilation over a couple of generations caused them to be recognised as Mancunians by the end of the century. The Irish were joined in the 1880s by Italians coming to find work, some in tile laying, some in the ice-cream and other street trades. They also settled in tightly knit communities but appear to have been greeted with much less hostility than the Irish earlier in the century. They turned the area around Blossom Street and Jersey Street into 'Little Italy', exotic to the outside observer with its annual Madonna procession and other festive events.

A *Times* reporter in 1819 had compared Ancoats to one of the 'rookeries' of early 19th-century London, and by the later 19th century, with the shift of London's problem districts further east, it was seen as the Mancunian equivalent of Bethnal Green or Whitechapel. In 1883 a Congregational minister, the Revd Andrew Mearns, published a sensational pamphlet, *The Bitter Cry of Outcast London*, exposing the squalid conditions of life for the poor in east London. It was echoed four years later by J H Crosfield's *The Bitter Cry of Ancoats and Impoverished Manchester*. Ancoats posed a social problem in need of a solution if its threats to public health and public order were to be averted.

Religious provision

Churches had been prominent in their attempts to find a solution. As early as 1821 the Methodists launched a mission to Ancoats and rapidly recruited followers to build a place of worship (Fig 41). Their work continued throughout the century. In 1897 the Methodist Mission opened the 'architecturally flamboyant' Victoria Hall as a base for its activities. Among community meeting rooms and offices, it housed a gymnasium, a photographic studio and a band practice room (Fig 42). Jactin House, a shelter for homeless men, was opened

Victoria Square. The quality of brickwork, ironwork and terracotta ornamentation, combined with the openness of the internal quadrangle, heralded a different world from the old Ancoats.
[DP058653]

Figure 41 (above, left)
Engraving of the Primitive Methodist Chapel, Jersey Street, 1832. It appears to show that the first place of worship in Ancoats, built c 1821 onwards, had converted (and extended vertically) a row of existing houses.
[Manchester Archives and Local Studies m10151]

Figure 42 (above, centre)
The Methodist Mission's Victoria Hall, shown here in 1897. The flamboyance of the architecture contrasts sharply with the sober Georgian treatment of the Methodists' first building.
[Manchester Archives and Local Studies m71900]

Figure 43 (left)
Round Chapel, Every Street, 1900. In 1823 James Scholefield, a radical Bible Christian, built this chapel which, by the end of the century, was to be the hub of the University Settlement social movement.
[Photo: A W Johnson. Manchester Archives and Local Studies, m08909]

Figure 44 (above)
St Peter's Church, Blossom Street , 1962. Built in 1859, on the site of a timber-yard and some housing in the very centre of Ancoats, the church was originally surrounded by houses and commercial premises.
[Photo: T Brooks 1962. Manchester Archives and Local Studies m10631]

Figure 45
A sister from Central Hall visiting the poor in 1893.
[Manchester Archives and Local Studies m68430]

Figure 46
Ardwick and Ancoats Dispensary. The early 19th-century
doorway of the Grade II listed historic hospital is a
reminder of its origins and it remains a part of the
building awaiting redevelopment.
[DP058506]

in 1891 and extended to front Murray Street in 1903, while the 'Derros Building', a handsome refuge for abused and 'fallen' women, was opened with a coffee tavern, at the corner of George Leigh Street and Great Ancoats Street in 1899. Two years after the first Methodist incursion, the radical Bible Christian James Scholefield built his Round Chapel on Every Street, at the eastern boundary of Ancoats (Fig 43). The established Anglican Church followed, with St Andrew's consecrated in 1831, All Souls in 1840 and St Philip's 10 years later. Then, perhaps a sign of alarm at the religious census of 1851 which showed the lack of both places of worship and worshippers in districts such as Ancoats, the magnificent Italianate Romanesque church of St Peter was built in 1859 in Blossom Street to the plans of the Manchester architect Isaac Holden (Fig 44). St Jude's and St Mark's followed in 1866 and 1884. The Roman Catholics provided for their faithful among the immigrant community: St Patrick's, Livesey Street, in 1832; St Anne's in 1847; and, in 1858, St Michael's, later the spiritual heart of Ancoats' Italian population.

These churches, and other societies of a non-sectarian nature, had their visitors to the poor. Well-meaning men and, more often, women went around the streets, knocking on doors and offering the poor inhabitants advice on cleanliness and godliness, together with a little, carefully assessed, material help in the shape of food, clothing or blankets. The reports which these explorers in Ancoats gave to their fellow churchgoers and members left no doubt as to the dire state of those visited (Fig 45).

Social enquiry and remedies

James Phillips Kay was a young doctor at the Ardwick and Ancoats Dispensary, a charitable institution for the treatment of the sick poor, founded in 1828 with George Murray as its president and James McConnel and John Kennedy as prominent subscribers (Fig 46). Kay's activity in treating the sick poor, especially during the serious cholera epidemic of 1832, led to the publication of his report, *The Moral and Physical Condition of the Working Classes Employed in the Cotton Manufacture in Manchester*. In this Kay pointed to the dangers of a mass of the poor, particularly Irish immigrants, crowded together in industrial suburbs such as Ancoats.

In 1833 Kay was, together with John Kennedy, a founder member of the Manchester Statistical Society, a body which devoted itself not to mathematical theory, but to social investigation. In 1865 its secretary, Henry Oats, carried out an 'Inquiry into the Educational and Other Conditions of a District in Ancoats'. Focusing on the area of earliest growth between Great Ancoats Street and New Islington, he produced a study which combined disturbing statistics (47 per cent of children in the area were neither in school nor in employment) with stomach-churning descriptions of overcrowded houses. Despite the efforts of the city council to improve drainage and paving in Ancoats, a survey in 1889 by Dr John Thresh for another investigative pressure group, the Manchester and Salford Sanitary Association, showed that Ancoats Number One District, the area of earliest housing development, had the second-highest infant mortality rate in the city. This he put down to the 'general dilapidation' of housing.

Figures 47 (left) and 48 (opposite)
Victoria Square, built in 1894–7. Still hugely imposing today, it must have contrasted dramatically with the mean houses around it in the 1890s.
[Detail from NMR 20786/14; DP058650]

Attempts had been made by philanthropists to remedy the housing problem. In 1881 the Manchester and Salford Workmen's Dwellings Company had built a block of two-roomed houses at Holt Town with, as Jacqueline Roberts records a century later, 'good sanitary arrangements, privacy and the possibility of decency in the domestic life of the tenants'. By the 1880s, however, it was becoming apparent that philanthropy was not enough. The state had to move in and provide housing rather than merely regulate its environment. In 1885 the city council formed an Unhealthy Dwellings Committee. The area of earliest housing in Ancoats, in the angle formed by Oldham Road and Great Ancoats Street and stretching to Bengal Street, was declared 'unhealthy'. A mass of back-to-back houses and insanitary courts were acquired and torn down, and a huge four-sided apartment block, Victoria Square, was built between 1894 and 1897 (p 46, Figs 47 and 48). Five storeys

high and with an open courtyard at its centre, it contained 235 two-roomed and 48 single-roomed flats. Each pair shared a lobby with cold-water tap, sink and WC. All were gas lit. Common laundries and drying rooms were provided in the corner turret towers. Across Spittal Street (Sherratt Street), rows of two-storey apartments were built along the initially named Sanitary (now Anita) Street, together with a row of three-bedroomed cottages on George Leigh Street (Figs 49, 50 and 51). These terraces, Victoria Square and the public

Figure 49 (opposite)
The densely packed courts of back-to-back housing of Primrose and Silk streets being replaced by the terraces of much higher quality housing of Anita Street and George Leigh Street, c 1898. The already completed Victoria Square can be seen in the background. [Manchester Archives and Local Studies m36543]

Figure 50 (above, left)
The Anita Street (formerly Sanitary Street) terraces of two-storey houses. [DP58509]

Figure 51 (above, right)
The three-storey terraces of George Leigh Street. [DP058519]

realm around them have recently been refurbished, and provide a prominent heritage backdrop to new developments in the area (*see* Chapter 7).

Despite their basic nature (Spalding and Cross, the architects of Victoria Square, installed concrete skirting boards and iron water-pipes lest tenants use wood for fires and lead to sell for scrap), many of these dwellings had rents too high for the casual Ancoats labourer. Families uprooted from the 'unhealthy area' had to crowd into cheaper, less sanitary accommodation.

Another report on housing conditions in Manchester and Salford (1904) still pointed to the inadequacies of much Ancoats housing. Its authors, Thomas Robert Marr and Thomas Coglan Horsfall, had two years earlier formed a Citizens' Association for the Improvement of the Unwholesome Dwellings and Surroundings of the People. The map of Manchester accompanying the report shows that in Ancoats all but a couple of back-to-back houses had been cleared or converted, but there were still large areas of slum properties. Indeed many of these around Rodney Street were to survive until a clearance order in 1959. Both Marr and Horsfall had close acquaintance with Ancoats. Marr was warden

of the Manchester University Settlement in Every Street, while Horsfall had
founded, in 1886, the Ancoats Art Museum in Ancoats Hall, the former home of
George Murray (Fig 52). In 1906 Marr was elected to represent the New Cross
Ward on the city council, and became chairman of its housing committee.

An earlier member of the city council, elected for New Cross in 1875, was
Charles Rowley, the Ancoats-born son of a picture framer. Rowley campaigned
for improvement in the condition of the people in Ancoats, and succeeded in
1880 in obtaining the building of New Islington Baths (Figs 53 and 54). His
ambition for Ancoats, however, went beyond clean clothes and bodies. He
argued that the grey, smoke-laden streets needed the light of culture, of music,
drama and works of art. He was a member of the committee, chaired by
Horsfall, which aimed to bring the arts to working people by means of the
Art Museum, displaying works of art and putting on lectures and concerts. It
would be available to all, with no entrance fee. Not content with this, Rowley
pursued his own means of bringing the light of culture to Ancoats. He formed
an Ancoats Recreation Committee at 78 Canning Street and at the New
Islington Hall, which he had persuaded the city council to build as a public

Figure 52
*Ancoats Hall, c 1900. George Murray's former home
was reused by the social reformer Thomas Coglan
Horsfall as an art gallery in 1886. It was closed as
a museum and art gallery in 1954 (see Fig 64).
[Photo: G E Anderton. Manchester Archives and Local
Studies m08910]*

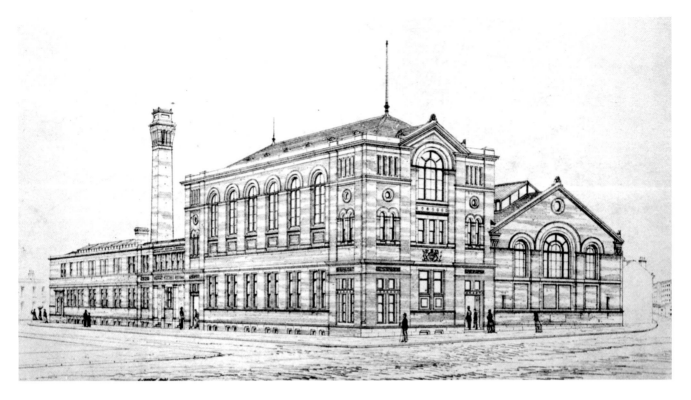

Figures 53 and 54
The New Islington Baths complex, built in 1880.
Observing the social mores of the time, it contained
first- and second-class swimming baths as well as a
female swimming bath (right).
[Manchester Archives and Local Studies m57408;
m57411]

Figure 55
Star Hall, Pollard Street, c *1900. From 1889 Francis*
Crossley, the noted manufacturer of gas engines,
developed a complex of social amenities, including
meeting rooms, washing baths and a 'coffee tavern'
as a rival to public houses.
[Manchester Archives and Local Studies m09994]

meeting place for Ancoats. The committee organised concerts, exhibitions and lectures by eminent people such as George Bernard Shaw, G K Chesterton and William Morris. The committee later developed into an Ancoats Brotherhood, with an ambitious programme of lectures and debates, together with organised rambles and cycling trips into the surrounding countryside. Such activities appealed to the educated artisan and the white-collar worker rather than to the mass of Ancoats people. In an effort to bridge the class gap more successfully and create an understanding of Ancoats life, Manchester University established a Settlement, based on the Toynbee Hall Settlement in east London, in 1895. Its aim was to provide residential accommodation for college-educated young men and women to give them the experience of living with working-class neighbours on an Ancoats street. Female residents shared lodgings in Ancoats Hall with the Art Museum, while men moved into 20 Every Street, beside the now somewhat dilapidated Round Chapel of the Revd Scholefield. From these bases the Settlement launched a range of activities, clubs, mothers' meetings, education classes and exhibitions. Residents also undertook social investigations into the lives of Ancoats people. One of the first of these was Marr and Horsfall's critical report of 1904 on Manchester and Salford housing.

A slightly earlier exponent of the 'settlement ideal' of the wealthy living alongside working people had been the gas engine manufacturer Francis Crossley. An evangelical Christian and admirer of the Salvation Army's founder, William Booth, he purchased the former Star music hall in Ancoats as a community meeting place with baths and a coffee room (Fig 55). In 1889, together with his wife, he left a comfortable home in Bowdon, south Manchester, to live at Star Hall. 'The Count Tolstoi of Manchester', proclaimed the *Liverpool Daily Post* on his death in 1897. Star Hall passed to the Salvation Army as a base for its mission work.

Activity of this sort, much of it created, controlled and financed by those outside Ancoats, had, by the early 20th century, created networks of support for the people. Part of its expression was in bricks and mortar, an architecture of social concern providing churches, schools, baths and washhouses, clubs, a gymnasium and meeting places. From the 1870s the Ardwick and Ancoats Dispensary had become Ancoats Hospital, with its expertise in the treatment of industrial accidents (Fig 56). Victoria Square and Anita Street bore witness to local government efforts to provide clean housing at a fair rent. Ancoats Hall, Star Hall and the Round Chapel had been transformed into social and cultural institutions, open to all. Ancoats people made use of these to varying degrees. However, they still found most support in their own institutions, pub, club and, above all, the informal network of family and neighbourhood. The 20th century was to prove unfriendly to these.

Figure 56
The Ardwick and Ancoats Dispensary, Old Mill Street.
Founded in 1828, it was developed into the Ancoats
Hospital in the 1870s. In the spring of 2011, Heritage
Works undertook an appraisal study to bring the building
back to life, shown here as it was in 2008, but its future
remains uncertain.
[DP058505]

6

Decline, a respite, then fall

In the first two decades of the 20th century the population of what the census authorities designated 'New Cross' stood at around 30,000. It had become a series of tight-knit communities, living in small terraced houses, their front doors opening onto cobbled streets. At one corner might be a small shop; at the other, perhaps a public house (Figs 57 and 58). Street, pub and family identified the individual as did church, chapel and ethnic origin. Whit week meant new clothes and processions (Protestants on Monday, Catholics on Friday) from Ancoats to Albert Square, marching behind the banner of their place of worship. Protestant and Catholic, Irish and Italian lived together in a fair degree of harmony. 'If they wanted to leave their children anywhere, the neighbours would be quite willing to oblige ... anybody sick would be well looked after', a former resident (b 1921) recalled for the Ancoats Buildings Preservation Trust's Oral History Project.

A brief dawn

The opening of a new council school, in George Leigh Street in 1912, brought up-to-date educational provision (Figs 59 and 60). Catering for children from the nursery age of 3 to the near universal leaving age of 14, it also provided shower baths for pupils whose homes lacked bathrooms or hot water, and a play centre for local children in out-of-school hours. A playground on the roof solved the problem of space in a densely inhabited area, though not that of retrieving a ball kicked over its high railings. The same year saw the Old Mill of 1797 rebuilt by McConnel and Kennedy to a much grander design (Fig 61). This, together with Murrays' New Little Mill on Jersey Street, was the first in the district to use electric power to drive spinning machinery. The power was supplied by its own dedicated municipal electricity substation designed by the city architect, Henry Lord (see Fig 70). In 1910 Alliot Roe, backed by his brother, Humphrey, began the manufacture of aeroplanes at the Brownsfield Mill. With the outbreak of war, the business found new customers and had to move to larger premises in Miles Platting and Newton Heath.

War in 1914 pulled many young men out of the community, some never to return. Military demands, and the absence of men, brought more, steadier and

Peel & Williams's Soho Foundry, 1957. Demolitions in the 1960s and 1970s included both Fairbairn's and Peel, Williams & Peel foundries.
[SER 8496, George Watkins Collection]

Figure 57
The Cross Keys, Jersey Street, 1962. The corner public
houses, once the social focus of the male community,
have mostly closed.
[Photo: T Brooks. Manchester Local Studies and
Archives m10189]

Figure 58
The Cross Keys, 2008. Overshadowed by the restored
Beehive Mill and Sankeys Soap nightclub, the pub is no
longer a social hub and the building is not in use.
[DP068552]

Figure 59
George Leigh Street School, built in 1912. The school's roof was its playground.
[DP070316]

Figure 60
George Leigh Street School interior, 2008. The high quality of the building is evidenced in the detail of this staircase.
[DP070269]

better-paid work for women in munitions and engineering as well as in cotton mills, many of which went over to the production of uniforms, tents, aircraft fabric and other such items. Supplies of raw cotton, which took up valuable shipping space, were rationed during the war by a Cotton Control Board, chaired by Sir Herbert Dixon, head of Fine Spinners and Doublers, into which Murrays' and McConnel & Co had been amalgamated in 1898. Despite the loss of overseas markets during the war, the Lancashire cotton industry indulged in an optimistic orgy of expansion after it. Dixon cautiously refused to involve Fine Spinners in this. As a result, McConnel's and Murrays' did not suffer as badly in the slump which engulfed the industry in the inter-war years. Manchester itself, given its greater range of industrial and commercial activity, did not experience the heavy unemployment of its neighbouring cotton towns.

Inter-war stagnation

Ancoats people, however, still experienced poverty. Cotton mills provided some employment for its women, but very little for its men. It remained an area dominated by unskilled casual labour. School leavers at 14 were too young for adult work or apprenticeship. To supplement the family income they seized what dead-end jobs were available. Boys found insecure, low-paid work as errand boys, van boys or cinema page-boys. Girls took jobs in the clothing trade, in box and paper-bag making or as cleaners. Moving from one job to another was not untypical, whether by choice or redundancy, in the harsh economic climate of the 1920s and 1930s. Railway companies with their goods yards at London Road and Oldham Road were a source of jobs which might include the care and driving of the horses pulling the delivery carts. Smithfield Market, on nearby Swan Street, provided opportunities for casual labour in fetching and carrying, loading and unloading.

In a scratch-as-scratch-can economy of this sort, where underemployment was perhaps as common as unemployment, the support of family and neighbours was vital. Church, chapel, mission and other philanthropic organisations also played supportive roles, not least in providing treats, entertainments and organised games for children to supplement informal, and at times risky, play in street, deserted building or canal. Terence, Kevin and Michael, the boy heroes of Malcolm Lynch's novel *The Streets of Ancoats* (1985), take part in Christmas activities at the Every Street Settlement, risking the wrath of Father Granelli at St Anne's, who condemned the Settlement as run by students who 'cut up dead bodies all day' and in the evenings advised 'the women of Ancoats about not having babies'. Religious differences were lightly observed when a free party or seaside outing was on offer at a rival church, chapel or club. Philanthropy also played a part in supplementing the minimal state relief of the 'dole' or in keeping families from the shame of having to enter the workhouse. More importantly, it helped to maintain morale in times of mental as well as economic depression. In 1931 the Settlement founded a Pilgrim Club for unemployed men. This provided occupational activity, carpentry or shoe repairing in the morning, cheap dinners, and organised sport, football or baseball in the afternoon. A membership fee of 2d was charged to avoid the stigma of charity.

Philanthropy could not help in solving Ancoats' most intractable problem, the housing of its people. The city council's policy of 'reconditioning' had made some improvements – WCs, cold-water supply and gas lighting – to the rows of 'two-up, two-down' terraces, many of them approaching their centenary. The fierce pride of Ancoats women in keeping the home respectable might disguise structural deficiencies. Window sills and doorsteps were 'donkey stoned', white at the front, brown at the back, and grids blackleaded. Friday night was remembered by some as 'bucket night', a thorough cleaning of hearth and home. By the end of World War I, however, few Ancoats houses were up to the new standards required as 'fit for heroes to live in'. Manchester's new council houses at Blackley, Wilbraham Road and later Wythenshawe had hot and cold water, small gardens and separate bedrooms for children of different sexes. Ancoats' 'brick boxes with slate lids' could not be brought up to this standard, and stood condemned as unfit for purpose. 'Slum clearance', the compulsory purchase and demolition of unfit homes, came onto the agenda, especially after the 1933 Housing Act, when central government would only subsidise new housing for those made homeless by clearance schemes.

Compulsory purchase and clearance schemes, such as the one drawn up in 1937 for streets lying between Pollard Street and the River Medlock, met with a mixed reaction from tenants. Most agreed that their old, decaying, verminous houses were not fit for pigs to live in; that they, and especially their children, would be healthier in the fresh air of Wythenshawe. On the other hand, rents would be higher, 15s a week compared with 7 or 8s in Ancoats. Jobs could not be found around the corner or a short walk away. Communities would be broken up. A bus ride (and fare) would be needed to visit a sick or aged relative still living in Ancoats. 'Slum' was a much-resented description of a house which they had improved and kept clean and respectable. Clearance and rehousing posed dilemmas beyond mere bricks and mortar and the economics of rent.

War in 1939 postponed the resolution of the situation. The Luftwaffe in its raids on Manchester in December 1940 might have brought with it a sudden and bloody form of slum clearance. Ancoats, however, was spared, despite the devastation of the nearby city centre. A stick of high explosive fell at the corner of Butler Street and Oldham Road, and two years later some bombs fell at the Beswick end of Palmerston Street, killing three people and seriously injuring seven. The shiny, modern Daily Express Building on Great Ancoats Street, opened in 1939, escaped unscathed (Fig 62, *see also* p 68, Figs 66 and 67). More devastating, as far as one section of the Ancoats community was concerned, was the official reaction to Italy's declaration of war on Britain in June 1940. Some 300 men from Italian families in Manchester were arrested by the police as potential enemy agents, despite the fact that some had sons or

Figure 62
Daily Express Building, Great Ancoats Street. Designed by Sir Owen Williams to print the northern edition of the paper and opened in 1939, it represented a hope of regeneration in a depressed area.
[Photo: L Kaye. Manchester Archives and Local Studies m11268]

nephews in the British army. A month later the *Arandora Star*, a ship carrying Italians and Germans to exile in Canada, was sunk by a German U-boat with the loss of nearly 500 Italian lives, many of whom were from Ancoats. Survivors were deported with other 'aliens' to the Isle of Man. Some did not return to Ancoats until after the war.

As in 1914, war brought jobs to Ancoats, with many of the mills going over to the production of war materials. During a morale-boosting visit to Manchester in 1942, George VI and Queen Elizabeth took a conducted tour of McConnel's mill, where an air-sea rescue dinghy being manufactured there was inflated in three minutes to their majesties' apparent delight. This short episode conferred upon McConnel's the title of 'Royal Mill' (Fig 63).

Post-war decline and dereliction

The post-war era brought no honours to Lancashire's cotton industry. A short-lived post-war boom turned to depression in the 1950s as Asian competition cut into its overseas and domestic markets. The 22 companies in Ancoats and Miles Platting listed in *Skinner's Cotton Trade Directory* for 1923 had fallen to 10 by 1953. Over the next decade the numbers employed in cotton nationally fell by 69 per cent, and the number of spindles active in Manchester and Salford by 88 per cent. Mills and smaller businesses were swallowed up in mergers, and by the 1960s cotton spinning in Ancoats had virtually ceased. Mills stood empty, or were let, floor by floor and room by room, to small business owners, many in the clothing and allied industries.

Meanwhile Ancoats' housing fell further behind national standards of fitness. By 1959, 68,000 houses in Manchester were described as 'grossly unfit'. In the 1960s compulsory purchase and clearance orders were issued for many Ancoats streets. Some houses were demolished; others were closed, bricked up and left to rot. Buildings central to Ancoats' history were also demolished. They included the New Islington Hall and Baths, Dr Scholefield's chapel on Every Street, and Ancoats Hall, the Horsfall Art Museum, next door (Fig 64). Commercial premises, clothing factories, warehouses, the famous Soho engineering works and Parker's timber-yard also fell to the wrecker's ball (p 58).

Figure 63
McConnel & Co's Old Mill, rebuilt in 1912. Its name was changed to Royal Mill in honour of a morale-boosting visit by the king and queen in 1942.
[DP058632]

As Granada TV's soap opera *Coronation Street*, launched in December 1960, became a national favourite, such streets were fast disappearing. The population of New Cross, half its 1921 size by 1951, fell still further. Residents moved out, some to Wythenshawe, others eastwards to Hyde and Hattersley to new, hygienic but rather soulless council estates. Attempts to recreate inner-city communities in Hulme, Ardwick and the 1970s 'Cardroom Estate' in New Islington met with mixed success. Schools such as George Leigh Street, their catchment areas denuded of children, closed. Churches lost their congregations, and were deconsecrated and closed. St Peter's, Blossom Street, shut its own doors, despite protests, in 1975, followed by St George's, Oldham Road, and St Paul's, New Cross, in 1981.

As the population fell, clothing manufacturers and other tenants of the Ancoats mills had to bus in workers from Wythenshawe to meet their labour needs. Then, finding huge mills like Murrays' inconvenient and expensive to operate, they moved out, leaving these symbols of the first Industrial Revolution empty and deteriorating. Wet and dry rot set in, weather and pigeons invaded, and squatters took up residence, some causing fires. The Bengal Street wing of Murrays' was so badly damaged by fire that it had to be demolished. The closure of the Daily Express Building in 1989 placed another iconic Ancoats building under threat. The pioneer industrial suburb seemed likely to return to its obscure, pre-industrial origins.

Figure 64
Ancoats Hall in ruins, 1964. Closed as a museum and
art gallery in 1954, Ancoats Hall was occupied by the
Ancoats branch of the British Railways Staff Association
prior to its demolition in the late 1960s.
[Photo: T Brooks. Manchester Archives and Local Studies
m47971]

7

History with a future

Julian Holder

Slowly – far too slowly for some buildings – realisation dawned that a physical presence of Manchester's history was in danger of disappearing. The final nail in the coffin was the closure of Express Printers in 1987 (opposite and Figs 65 and 66). This took away not only the jobs of the printers but the livelihoods of those local shops, cafes and pubs that relied on its existence for their own survival (Figs 67 and 68). Although the building it was housed in, Owen Williams' prepossessing Daily Express Building, had been listed as early as 1974, this recognition was a rare exception in an area with only four listed buildings.

Appreciation, designation and change

In the 1980s, despite many years of effort by an energetic and vocal conservation lobby, the industrial archaeology of the area was still not readily understood by those decision-makers in whose hands its future lay. The emergency recording of vulnerable buildings had already revealed the exceptional interest of many of the buildings in the area, but only now was to inform a listing campaign. Within a year of the closure of the Daily Express another 11 buildings – mainly mills – were listed, and in June 1989 Manchester City Council designated a conservation area. Bounded chiefly by the Rochdale Canal, Great Ancoats Street, Oldham Road and Kemp Street, it effectively also redefined and rebranded what was historic Ancoats – the surviving remnant of a much greater area.

The listings were important, as this was the first time that the historic character of the whole landscape was recognised as being important within the planning system. Like many historic areas Ancoats is much more than a collection of buildings (Fig 69). A statement of hope for the future, the conservation area status ensured that any proposals for demolition, not just of the listed buildings, were carefully considered. It also ensured that options for the reuse of the unlisted redundant buildings were actively pursued (Fig 70). In short, it gave Ancoats, with a decayed infrastructure, a depleted community and an uncertain future, a fighting chance.

Without this the area could have quickly fallen prey to the demolition contractors' balls, as Manchester's bid to host the 2000 Olympics brought its own development pressures. Although it contains the most important surviving

*Daily Express Building, Great Ancoats Street.
[DPO58564]*

Figures 65 and 66
Daily Express Building, Great Ancoats Street. This was designated a historic building in 1974 as a fine example of 1930s architecture.
[DP058566; DP058554]

Figure 67 (below)
38 Great Ancoats St. Ancoats is characterised not merely by contrasts of style but also size as these modest commercial premises next door to the giant Hudson Buildings demonstrate. Great Ancoats Street has always been an area of mixed commercial premises fronting the industrial district behind.
[DP058503]

Figure 68 (right)
Blossom St. A view looking into Blossom Street with the Ice Plant building awaiting its redevelopment.
[DP070255]

Figure 69
The iron kerbs, gratings, makers' plates and plaques impart so much character to the conservation area.

This page, clockwise
Reproduction fly wheel, Royal Mill [DP058610]; maker's plate, Henry Street canal bridge [DP068560]; nameplate on weighbridge, Murrays' Mills [DP058612]; canal bollard [DP068557]; metal kerb, Primrose Street [DP070237]

Opposite page, clockwise
Date stone, Coates School, Jersey Street [DP058534]; leaded lights, 'Derros Building' [DP070214]; stonework at canal bridge, east end of Jersey Street [DP068526]; factory bell, Murrays' Mills [DP070283]; iron drain cover, Primrose Street [DP070234]; nameplate, Union Street bridge, Rochdale Canal [DP068535]

Figure 70
The unusually grand former electricity substation, with adjacent council housing for the workers, was built in 1911 to power Paragon Mill and Royal Mill.
[DP070206]

collection of steam-powered mills in England, their deteriorating condition was also a symbol of the post-industrial collapse of the country during a period of rapid economic change. Many saw them as merely an embarrassment and an impediment to Manchester's attempts to find a new post-industrial role which the Olympic bid offered, and which the commercial success of the nearby Central Retail Park seemed to confirm. The skill of those concerned with the future of Ancoats was to ensure that any new developments could work with the old, and maintain the strong and varied character of the place at the same time.

One of the immediate effects of obtaining conservation area status was to make this historic fabric eligible for a Conservation Area Partnership grant from English Heritage. Manchester City Council and English Heritage worked together in supporting sympathetic owners prepared to invest in the dream of a revived Ancoats. This provided small grants for essential holding and enveloping works, rectified unsympathetic alterations and restored the historic character of the buildings. In this way defective gutters were replaced, buildings made secure against both the elements and vandalism, and small

Figure 71 (opposite, top)
Beehive Mill. Since the early phase in its rehabilitation its use has included a nightclub, Sankeys Soap.
[DP070276]

Figure 72 (opposite, bottom)
Detail of gas light, Crown & Kettle public house (see Fig 100). On the New Cross corner of Great Ancoats Street and Oldham Road, the pub was the original meeting place of Ancoats Buildings Preservation Trust and retains some early features.
[DP058543]

pockets of the area revealed to be worth a second look. The need for a second look was confirmed with the publication, in 1992, of a major survey of the cotton mills of Greater Manchester by Williams and Farnie in association with the Greater Manchester Archaeological Unit and the Royal Commission on the Historical Monuments of England. Building on the work in the 1980s, this new research greatly increased our understanding, and not only demonstrated the importance of mill buildings nationally but reaffirmed the importance of those in Ancoats on the international stage.

Conservation-led regeneration

Crucial to the regeneration of Ancoats was the establishment in 1995 of the Ancoats Buildings Preservation Trust. A charitable trust established by volunteers, it was part of the larger movement of preservation trusts which take on buildings beyond the economic capabilities of the private sector. Ancoats was one of the earliest to be working in a run-down inner-city area, and given the scale of the buildings in question, certainly one of the most ambitious. Its establishment coincided with a national, and somewhat heated, conference on the top floor of the recently converted Beehive Mill (*see* Figs 20 and 21). The conference was held following the inception of a new listing programme for mill buildings, and this beautifully refurbished building, complete with an emblematic Manchester nightclub in the basement – Sankeys Soap (Fig 71) – was a powerful demonstration of the reuse of such buildings at a time when their deteriorating condition, lack of statutory protection and increasing redundancy were leading to significant losses up and down the country, not merely in Manchester.

The Trust met originally in the Crown & Kettle (Figs 72 and 100) on Great Ancoats Street, and within a few years found itself responsible for St Peter's Church (Figs 73, 74 and 75) and Murrays' Mills (Fig 76), both of which were vital to the future of Ancoats. Trading on goodwill, enthusiasm and wide professional support, this group of volunteers quickly developed an impetus that brought the plight of Ancoats to the public's attention. It secured the listing of the 'Derros Building' in 1998, and was soon supported by an active Friends organisation (Fig 77). While arson attacks continued, dereliction and

Figure 73
St Peter's Church, Blossom Street. The restoration by
Ancoats Buildings Preservation Trust of key buildings
such as St Peter's was a crucial step in the regeneration
of the area, as was that of the adjacent Jactin House.
[NMR 20786/11]

decay still hung in the air, but there was a sense that the situation could be reversed. However, if this was to come about then as much effort had to be put into making the area sustainable as into the conservation of its unique character. The creation of the Ancoats Urban Village Company in 1996 helped to steer commercial development to that end. Part of the wider regeneration of Manchester Eastside, it worked to ensure that Ancoats would become an attractive place to live, work and play (Figs 78 and 79).

Responding to the close-knit Italian community that had occupied the area around St Peter's Church known as 'Little Italy', the Trust and the Company promoted the image of Ancoats reborn as an urban village. Long cut off and isolated from the city centre by the traffic on Great Ancoats Street, Ancoats with its enclosed nature lent itself to such an experiment, which demanded an

Figures 74 and 75
The restored interior of St Peter's Church and a detail
of one of the lights.
[DP058642; DP058644]

Figure 76
The huge complex of Murrays' Mills. Ancoats Buildings Preservation Trust's biggest challenge was its restoration, which was accomplished in 2007, complete with the courtyard canal basin.
[NMR 20788/55]

area with a mix of different uses that could be easily walked across in 10 minutes or so, gave priority to pedestrians and retained a strong sense of community. Based on the concepts of a public square centred on the church (*see* Frontispiece), the conversion of Jactin House and the former Ice Plant building, along with new housing, shops and services to tempt people back to Ancoats – and city-centre living generally – a vision for the future was finally agreed. Ancoats having been celebrated as the world's first suburb of the Industrial Revolution, it was appropriate that another seeming contradiction, an urban village, should have been arrived at to secure its future.

However, any objective assessment of the situation Ancoats found itself in recognised that protective measures, a building preservation trust run by dedicated professional volunteers and a new vision alone were not enough to guarantee the longer-term sustainability of the area. It could only thrive once again if the larger, seemingly intractable buildings, such as the enormous Royal Mill complex and Murrays' Mills, were put into good repair, adapted and reused (Fig 80). One of the biggest impediments to regeneration remained the multiplicity of small building owners, often hard to locate; the total was once believed to be in excess of 200. Many of these were speculators sitting on

Figure 77
The 'Derros Building'. The women's refuge and coffee house of 1899 have been given a new lease of life as offices. The multi-storey car park behind has been designed to blend in with its surroundings.
[DP070248]

Figures 78 and 79
The Hudson Buildings. Conversion of properties such as this and the 'Derros Building', along with the refurbishment of the Daily Express Building, has restored some of the prestige to Great Ancoats Street.
[DP058574; DP070251]

neglected property in advance of Manchester's bid for the Olympic and then Commonwealth Games, until their development value could be realised. It became clear that without large-scale co-ordinated action regeneration was likely to stall, if it ever went beyond a few key buildings such as St Peter's.

The solution was the acquisition, through compulsory purchase, of large tracts of Ancoats by the Northwest Regional Development Agency (NRDA). With the close cooperation of other agencies – such as the New East Manchester Urban Development Company and especially the Ancoats Urban Village Company, which played a leading role – this action gave Manchester City Council the confidence not only to issue supplementary planning guidance in 1999 but also to put attractive high-quality public realm in place, involving better paving materials, careful consideration of traffic movements and signage, lighting schemes, and maintenance of those parts of the public realm which were of value, such as the characteristic iron kerbs (Figs 69 and 81).

With the help of Single Regeneration Budget money from the City Council, NRDA funding, grant from English Heritage, and especially the sizeable grants which became available from the Heritage Lottery Fund, the momentum increased. Meanwhile, on the other side of the city, the successful regeneration of the Castlefield canal basin showed what was possible, with a mixture of sensitive adaptation of listed buildings and carefully integrated new developments to restore confidence. Its historical link, via the Rochdale Canal supplying the coal to power Ancoats' mills, and a return route for its products, suggested a bid for World Heritage status, which immediately lifted Ancoats from being merely a run-down former industrial part of Manchester to an area of universal significance. With its inclusion in the UK Tentative List of World Heritage Sites in 1999, the claim to be the pioneer suburb of the Industrial Revolution was validated. The opening first of the extension to the Daily Express Building in 2001, with a mixture of apartments and offices in an industrial style to complement the original, and then of Waulk Mill in 2002, after an extensive programme of restoration and adaptation to offices, proved what could be achieved.

Figure 80
The group of preserved mills to the west of the Rochdale Canal contrasts sharply with the areas of historic Ancoats to the east of the canal which are being developed as part of the New Islington project.
[NMR20792/21]

Figure 81 (opposite)
Redhill Street canal locks. Once a source of hazard and pollution, the canal is now embraced by the public realm.
[DP068561]

Combining the old with the new

More recently the wider regeneration of the surrounding area, especially the Northern Quarter and the creation of the Millennium Village of New Islington has encouraged the regeneration of Ancoats to take a different turn and feed off its wider regenerative effect (Fig 82). No longer is the concept of the urban village which informed its development through the 1990s quite so central – Ancoats' canal arms are re-opening in Cotton Field allowing development to push down to New Islington, Holt Town and beyond to the Ashton Canal. Some of the services necessary to support the urban village will simply reproduce those now found elsewhere. If the urban village concept has gone, it has only given way to the idea of 'the Heart of Ancoats', itself an early concept for the regeneration of the area, centred on the newly restored St Peter's Church (*see* Frontispiece), with a public square as a central meeting place for the new community as it establishes itself. Originally set to grow from a population of 900 to over 7,000 in the coming years, the proposed growth, and the timescale within which this may happen, has, however, been affected by the altered economic circumstances since 2008.

The conversion of the Royal Mill complex to a mixed-use development providing over 100 apartments, together with retail and office accommodation, was a major demonstration that the regeneration of Ancoats was succeeding and, time has shown, this is continuing despite the financial crisis (inside front cover, Figs 83, 84 and 85). Shielded from public view by the mills, the various components of this complex, including Sedgwick and Paragon mills, are tied together by a magnificent new glass atrium which encloses the former courtyard, and has allowed the insertion of a new business centre. Old and new co-exist happily while sharing the same industrial aesthetic. Further along the iconic canal frontage, and physically connected to Royal Mill by the slenderest of high-level bridges, the equally complex range of buildings which constitute Murrays' Mills has been repaired and restored, and these await their first residents, once converted to flats. In this sense Ancoats acts as something of a barometer for the changes in the market for residential accommodation in and around the city centre.

It was developments such as MMII, completed in 2003, which began the insertion of new buildings into this historic area. Responding to the general height, massing, materials and solidity of the mills along the Rochdale Canal, this first new major building of apartments, live/work units and shops in Ancoats since the decline of the area established an approach for others to build upon – a challenge met by the new extensions to Royal Mill. Nearby a new brick-faced multi-storey car park also preserves this important aspect of the area, and manages to slip seamlessly into the tall canyon of buildings alongside its muscular industrial cousins (Fig 86).

Where MMII aped the predominantly brick idiom of Ancoats, later developments – such as 41 Bengal Street, opened in 2008 – have begun to introduce a more contemporary feel in areas only slightly less sensitive than those which front Redhill Street (Fig 87). Here the architects, while following the advice in the supplementary planning guidance, have reworked the typology of a mill building in terms of its eight-storey height and mass by

Figure 82
The vibrant and playful Islington Square housing scheme, designed by FAT, sits on the edge of Ancoats providing 23 new homes for the Manchester Methodist Housing Association.
[DP136580]

Figures 83 (left), 84 (below) and 85 (opposite)
The beating 'Heart of Ancoats', McConnel's mills. Behind the unchanged canal frontage of Royal and Sedgwick mills lies a world of apartments, offices and an arcade of shops linked by a glazed atrium.
[DP058598; DP058601; DP058635]

sitting a crisp white rendered building on top of a heavy, dark podium (Fig 88). The 'shock of the new' about the building is not so much the departure from brick to white render as the four-storey square cut-out in the middle of the building (Fig 89). This not only adds a dramatic element to the new building, making it 'of its time', but affords views through, while giving some of the residents of its 48 flats partially enclosed balconies where they can sit semi-cocooned in the cut-out – literally providing a window on history.

Figure 86
Blending the new with the old. An occasional
factory chimney still dominates canyons of old and
new buildings.
[DP058618]

Ancoats, while staying true to its historic character, must find a home for well-conceived new buildings if it is both to be reanimated and to connect with the new architecture beginning to complement the area on its fringes. New developments such as Islington Square (*see* Fig 82) and Chips (Figs 90 and 91), whilst not to everyone's tastes, introduce a note of gaiety to the surrounding area that tempt new visitors to Ancoats and help regeneration. In addition, smaller developers, beginning to put their trust in Ancoats, have begun to refurbish and rework buildings such as 2–4 Loom Street, parts of the German Warehouses (Figs 92 and 93), the Flint Glass Works (Fig 94) and 46 Radium Street – now named 'Sam's Foundry'. The colourful polychromatic brickwork of the German Warehouses stands out in an area otherwise characterised by the quite dignity and sobriety of its materials. So much of the character of Ancoats derives not simply from its giant, gaunt mill buildings but its smaller incidental buildings such as these. They are the buildings, too easily overlooked, which create the dramatic contrasts of scale in the area and which speak eloquently of the whole community and its history, not only the mills, dominant though they may be. Without them the area becomes one-dimensional and tells but a partial story. Without them we cannot ask the inevitable questions the area poses – where did the people that worked here

Figure 87 (above)
The new office and apartment block designed by MBLA architects sits comfortably next to one of Ancoats' older buildings on Radium Street.
[DP058661]

Figures 88 and 89 (left and opposite)
No. 41 Bengal Street. A contemporary building with the same massing as adjacent mills and the former school, but with a very different finish, complements its neighbours. The central cut-out with views beyond visually links the historic buildings on either side.
[NMR 20785/15; DP058619]

Figures 90 and 91 (left and above)
The Chips building designed by Will Alsop and completed in 2009 uses enlarged newspaper print as decoration as a reminder of the printing heritage of Ancoats. On the boundary of Greater Ancoats, it is close to the Ashton Canal and its associated historic locks, buildings and bridges. [DP136568; DP136572]

Figures 92 and 93 (opposite, above)
German Warehouses. Many of the smaller buildings in the conservation area are now attracting developers. Whilst the colourful German Warehouses on George Leigh Street await new uses, to the rear, in Silk Street, they are already being progressively converted in an imaginative way. [DP058655; DP070330]

Figure 94 (opposite, left)
The Flint Glass Works, Jersey Street. [DP070272]

Figure 95 (opposite, right)
George Leigh Street School. Offices and the boardroom of Ask Property Developments Limited have been built onto the former roof playground of the school. [DP058538]

livc, and how did they live? Where did they eat, sleep, play, love and worship? How do we remember them? Crucially for regeneration, once adapted to new uses, buildings such as these allow the provision of important new services, for example the doctor's surgery now operating out of Sam's Foundry – a small former warehouse – or the new offices fitted into the rear of the German Warehouses and in the former George Leigh Street School (Fig 95).

Other community outreach and arts initiatives have served to maintain and extend the life of Ancoats. Organised by Ancoats Buildings Preservation Trust, 'Skills, Schools, Stories' was a programme designed to provide opportunities for people of all ages to get involved in the restoration of Murrays' Mills and the regeneration of the Ancoats area (Figs 96 and 97). With £150,000 of funding from the Heritage Lottery Fund, private-sector sponsorship and 'contributions in kind' from volunteers, the project ran workshops and site visits for schoolchildren, skills tasters for young people and

Figures 96 and 97
Murrays' Mills. The restored mills and one of the fine stone staircases ready for use.
[DP070286; DP058617]

Figure 98
George Leigh Street School. The roof playground
spy-hole of the school presages the Peeps spy-holes of
a century later.
[DP070265]

an oral history project. In terms of public art, items found during the course of restoration work, often walled up in buildings as they expanded, became an object of fascination for artist Dan Dubowitz. Like many others initially drawn to the plight of the area, he had already taken photographs of derelict Ancoats. With the example of the walled-up objects before him, Dubowitz created a public artwork, called *The Peeps*, comprising a series of spy-holes around Ancoats through which historic objects can be seen. Some of these, such as 'Serafino's Stone' next to Victoria Square, are obvious, others less so, but all give an insight into the idea of the private, and partially forgotten, world which was Ancoats (Figs 98 and 99), whilst his large photographs, displayed in the Cutting Room Square sculpture panels or 'sentinels', show the dereliction which once beset the area (*see* Frontispiece).

In retrospect what was one of the worst days for Ancoats, the closure of Express Printers, was also one of its best. The Daily Express Building, which seemed to signal the end of Ancoats, has now been excitingly and respectfully adapted and extended to provide new jobs and places to live. The Crown & Kettle, one of the early casualties of the closure of Express Printers, is once again trading as the community is rebuilt (Fig 100).

Today key buildings which give the area its identity and distinctiveness, such as St Peter's Church and Murrays' Mills, have been restored and await new uses as evidence of Ancoats' success. It has been a long struggle that altered not only buildings but people's lives, and the city's and region's image of themselves in the process. Thankfully, while the financial crisis has slowed progress and much remains to be done, 20 years after Express Printers closed, Ancoats can truly be said to have not only a history, but a history with a future.

Figure 99
The Peeps – 'Serafino's Stone'. Serafino di Felice, a leading member of the Ancoats Italian community, was an early trustee of Ancoats Buildings Preservation Trust.
[DP058638]

Figure 100
The Crown & Kettle. Now restored, the pub caters for a different, but still local, community.
[DP058546]

References

Adshead, 1851 *Adshead's Twenty-four Illustrated Maps of the Township of Manchester Divided into Municipal Wards*. Manchester: Joseph Adshead

Ancoats Buildings Preservation Trust Oral History Project 1956 *All Work and No Play?* Transcript ID7-23.56. Recordings stored at North West Sound Archive, Clitheroe, Lancs.

Anon 1851 *The Great Exhibition, London 1851: Illustrated Catalogue of the Industry of All Nations* (facsim edn David & Charles 1970, 290)

Axon, W E A 1883 *Manchester Gleanings*. Manchester: Tubbs, Brook, & Chrystal; London: Simpkin, Marshall & Co

Baines, E 1835 *History of the Cotton Manufacture in Great Britain*. London

Bancks & Co 1832 *Plan of Manchester and Salford. with their Environs*. Manchester: Bancks & Co

Bindman, D and Riemann, G (eds) 1993 *Karl Friedrich Schinkel. The English Journey: Journal of a Visit to France and Britain in 1826*. New Haven and London: Yale University Press

Bruton, F A 1924 *A Short History of Manchester and Salford*. Manchester: Sherratt & Hughes

Engels, F 1845 *The Condition of the Working Class in England in 1844*. (1987 edn, Kiernan V (ed). Penguin Classics). Harmondsworth: Penguin, 95 and 96

Green, W 1794 *Plan of Manchester and Salford Drawn from an Actual Survey by William Green*. [Manchester]

Gregory, L 2007 'Under slate grey Victorian sky'. MA dissertation, University of Manchester

Johnson, W 1819 *Plan of the Parish of Manchester in the County of Lancaster*.

Kay, J P 1832 *The Moral and Physical Condition of the Working Classes Employed in the Cotton Manufacture in Manchester*. (Facsim reprint of 2nd edn, Manchester: E J Morten 1969), 55

Kennedy, B 1905 *Slavery: Pictures from the Depths*. London: Anthony Treherne, 80

Laurent, C 1793 *A Topographical Plan of Manchester and Salford: Shewing Also the Different Allotments of Land Proposed to Be Built On, as Communicated to the Surveyor by the Respective Proprietors*. [London]: C Laurent

Marr, T R 1904 *Housing Conditions in Manchester and Salford. A Report prepared for the Citizens Association for the Improvement of the Unwholesome Dwellings and Surroundings of the People*. Manchester: Sherratt & Hughes; University Press, Frontispiece

McConnell & Co Ltd 1913 *A Century of Fine Spinning, Ancoats, Manchester 1790–1913*, 2 edn. Manchester: George Falkner & Sons

Oats, H C 1865/6 'Inquiry into the educational and other conditions of a district in Ancoats: Report of the Committee'. (Read at a meeting of the Society held November 15, 1865) *Transactions of the Manchester Statistical Society*, 5

Ginswick, J (ed) 1983 *Labour and the Poor in England and Wales, 1849–1851: The letters to the* Morning Chronicle *from the Correspondents in the Manufacturing and Mining Districts, the Towns of Liverpool and Birmingham, and the Rural Districts, Vol I: Lancashire, Cheshire, Yorkshire*. London: Frank Cass, 19

Roberts, J 1993 'The residential development of Ancoats'. *Manchester Region History Review VII*, 24

Thresh, J C 1889–90 'An enquiry into the causes of the excessive mortality in No. 1 District, Ancoats' (Paper read to Manchester and Salford Sanitary Association, May 30 1889) *Public Health* **2**, 17

Further reading

Dubowitz, D 2003 *Wastelands, Vol I: Ancoats*. Manchester: Civic Works

Dubowitz, D 2011 *The Peeps. Ancoats: The Presence of Absence*. Manchester: Manchester University Press

Hartwell, C 2001 *Manchester*. London: Penguin

Heritage Works Buildings Preservation Trust 2007 *All Work & No Play? An Ancoats Scrapbook*. Manchester: Heritage Works Buildings Preservation Trust

Hylton, S 2003 *A History of Manchester*. Chichester: Phillimore

Kidd, A 2002 *Manchester*, 3 edn. Edinburgh: Edinburgh University Press

Kidd, A and Wyke, T (eds) 1993 *Ancoats: The First Industrial Suburb*. (Manchester Region History Review **7**, special issue)

McNeil, R and George, D (eds) 2002 *Manchester – Archetype City of the Industrial Revolution: A Proposed World Heritage Site* (Heritage Atlas 4). Manchester: University of Manchester, Field Archaeology Centre

McNeil, R and Stevenson, M (eds) 1996 *Textile Legacy* (Heritage Atlas 2). Manchester: University of Manchester, Field Archaeology Centre

Miller, I *et al* 2007 *A & G Murray and the Cotton Mills of Ancoats* (Lancaster Imprints 13). Lancaster: Oxford Archaeology North

Williams, M with Farnie, D A 1992 *Cotton Mills in Greater Manchester*. Preston: Carnegie

Other titles in the Informed Conservation series

Behind the Veneer: The South Shoreditch furniture trade and its buildings.
Joanna Smith and Ray Rogers, 2006.
Product code 51204, ISBN 9781873592960

Berwick-upon-Tweed: Three places, two nations, one town.
Adam Menuge with Catherine Dewar, 2009.
Product code 51471, ISBN 9781848020290

The Birmingham Jewellery Quarter: An introduction and guide.
John Cattell and Bob Hawkins, 2000.
Product code 50205, ISBN 9781850747772

Bridport and West Bay: The buildings of the flax and hemp industry.
Mike Williams, 2006.
Product code 51167, ISBN 9781873592861

Building a Better Society: Liverpool's historic institutional buildings.
Colum Giles, 2008.
Product code 51332, ISBN 9781873592908

Built to Last? The buildings of the Northamptonshire boot and shoe industry.
Kathryn A Morrison with Ann Bond, 2004.
Product code 50921, ISBN 9781873592793

Defending Scilly.
Mark Bowden and Allan Brodie, 2011.
Product code 51530, ISBN 9781848020436

England's Schools: History, architecture and adaptation.
Elain Harwood, 2010.
Product code 51476, ISBN 9781848020313

English Garden Cities: An introduction.
Mervyn Miller, 2010.
Product code 51532, ISBN 9781848020511

Gateshead: Architecture in a changing English urban landscape.
Simon Taylor and David Lovie, 2004.
Product code 52000, ISBN 9781873592762

Manchester's Northern Quarter.
Simon Taylor and Julian Holder, 2008.
Product code 50946, ISBN 9781873592847

Manchester: The warehouse legacy – An introduction and guide.
Simon Taylor, Malcolm Cooper and P S Barnwell, 2002.
Product code 50668, ISBN 9781873592670

Manningham: Character and diversity in a Bradford suburb.
Simon Taylor and Kathryn Gibson, 2010.
Product code 51475, ISBN 9781848020306

Newcastle's Grainger Town: An urban renaissance.
Fiona Cullen and David Lovie, 2003.
Product code 50811, ISBN 9781873592779

'One Great Workshop': The buildings of the Sheffield metal trades.
Nicola Wray, Bob Hawkins and Colum Giles, 2001.
Product code 50214, ISBN 9781873592663

Ordinary Landscapes, Special Places: Anfield, Breckfield and the growth of Liverpool's suburbs.
Adam Menuge, 2008.
Product code 51343, ISBN 9781873592892

Plymouth: Vision of a modern city.
Jeremy Gould, 2010.
Product code 51531, ISBN 9781848020504

Stourport-on-Severn: Pioneer town of the canal age.
Colum Giles, Keith Falconer, Barry Jones and Michael Taylor, 2007.
Product code 51290, ISBN 9781905624362

Further information on titles in the Informed Conservation series can be found on our website.

To order through EH Sales
Tel: 0845 458 9910
Fax: 0845 458 9912
Email: eh@centralbooks.com
Online bookshop: www.english-heritageshop.org.uk

Map of the Ancoats Conservation Area, and its environs, showing key sites

1 Jackson's Warehouse and canal basin
2 Rochdale Canal, Tariff Street bridge
3 Rochdale Canal, Brownsfield Mill, lock 83
4 Brownsfield Mill
5 Rochdale Canal, Great Ancoats Street bridge and lock 82
6 Rochdale Canal, Union Foundry footbridge
7 MMII building
8 McConnel & Kennedy's Mill, Royal Mill
9 McConnel & Kennedy's Mill, Sedgwick Mill, main block
10 McConnel & Kennedy's Mill, Sedgwick Mill, west wing
11 McConnel & Kennedy's Mill, Sedgwick Mill, east wing
12 McConnel & Kennedy's Mill, Sedgwick Mill, new mill
13 McConnel & Kennedy's Mill, Paragon Mill
14 Paragon Mill and Royal Mill, electricity substation and associated housing
15 Murrays' Mills, Old Mill
16 Murrays' Mills, Decker Mill
17 Murrays' Mills, Murray Street Warehouse
18 Murrays' Mills, New Mill
19 Murrays' Mills, New Little Mill
20 Murrays' Mills, Doubling Mill and Fireproof Mill
21 Murrays' Mills, canal basin

22 British & Foreign Flint Glass Works
23 Former Jersey Street Mill
24 Islington Square
25 Cotton Field
26 Rochdale Canal, Union Street bridge
27 Rochdale Canal, former bridge over branch canal, Jersey Street
28 Rochdale Canal, former bridge over branch canal, Poland Street
29 German Warehouses
30 Beehive Mill
31 Cross Keys public house
32 George Leigh Street School (Ask building)
33 No. 41 Bengal Street
34 Jactin House
35 St Peter's Church
36 Cutting Room Square
37 Ice Plant Building
38 Victoria Square
39 Anita Street
40 Nos 44–68 Oldham Road
41 Nos 23–57 George Leigh Street
42 Loom Street plots, disused
43 St Michael's Church
44 Hudson Buildings
45 'Derros Building'
46 Daily Express Building
47 Daily Express Building, 2001 extension
48 Crown & Kettle public house
49 New Cross